MYSTICS

THE THIRD POWER

BY

JAKE PIXLEY

Printed in the United States of America.
Send all inquiries to:
authorjakepixley@gmail.com

OTHER BOOKS BY JAKE PIXLEY:

Across The Plane (Tom Carpenter's Journey)

The Candy Profile

Mystics

Mystics (The Two Powers)

CHAPTER 1

The death of Evelyn Murray brought with it the wrath and determination of the mystics. Her sacrifice inspired a new determination to once and for all, rid the world of Luciftias and Shadow.

Lundar and Theodess presented their plan to unite Anglamora with Danann to Katie Carpenter, currently known as the keeper of the white staff.

Katie accepted the plan and Lundar assembled a small fellowship of his men including Theodess and Tanamit. The reaper Badru joined them, as they began on their nervous journey east to see King Darr of the Tuatha De' Danann.

King Eshnar of Locklure ordered his druids to the Eastern Mountain where the border of their land connected to Anglamora.

"Here we will build three horns on watch towers. One for wrath, one for ruin, and one to unite us all." Eshnar said to the druids standing with him.

One horn for the gathering of forces. One horn for the retreat to the next land. The chief horn designed to equal the knell of Anitoll. It was to never be heard unless Evelyn made a return.

At the great tomb in the center of the eternal cemetery, the Undertaker stood alone at the foot of the sarcophagus of Evelyn Murray, while holding a large double bit axe. Luke and the Grave Digger stood on each side. All of them were dressed in black leather armor as they prepared for war.

In Anglamora, six of the reapers stayed by Katie's side at all times. None in Anglamora believed Luciftias would hold his end of the bargain. War for the mystics was once again only a matter of time.

Luciftias was focused on the people of Danann. Shadow crept in that land and corrupted the minds of many. Division among the masses led to fights, conspiracies and a half population seeking to overthrow King Darr.

He was known as the slayer of worhawks. His crown made from their talons. King Darr, the keeper of the philosophers' stone, prepared his loyal forces for battle. He was prepared to stand alone against the evil that swept his land.

The Grim Reaper and the great wandering star of Anglamora, Aerenthia were entering the box canyon. The home of the Timekeeper.

Fate, Destiny and Karma had gathered on top of the stony black mountain of Locklure. From there they focused on their sight to the ice wall miles away.

Not far from the trio of deities, a pecan shell hit the ground, followed by a bare foot over the rocks. The Mediator joined the other three and looked to the distant ice wall.

"Locklure is neutral ground," the Mediator said to them.

Destiny replied. "Not much longer."

As the others looked to the north at the distant ice wall, Destiny looked to her left as she wondered about John Porter and the Timekeeper.

Aerenthia and John had found the secret passage down the high bluffs into the canyon. The passage was a mere bear trail from many years of use.

It began in a crack in the bluff only a couple feet wide and going down at an angle. Then it stopped and turned the opposite direction through another crack in the bluff stone.

If not for the Timekeeper having lined the small trail with stone, it would be unidentifiable. At the bottom of the bluff below the canopy of the tall trees, the valley floor was exposed to them.

The valley was riddled with moss covered boulders, mountain streams and wild herbs planted in rows like a garden.

John only took a moment to take in the beauty of the valley before he took off walking. That's when Aerenthia stopped him.

"John, look at this." She said to him.

He turned around and looked upon the bluff face that was covered in paintings of clocks. The words, "3 seconds" repeated in various languages below each clock.

"What do you think Aerenthia, is it obsession or insanity?"

She turned to look at Him but never spoke. Instead, she joined him in walking further into the valley toward a small distant smoke column.

It wasn't long before John Porter and Aerenthia found themselves approaching a lean two shack made from nearby trees and roofed with a bed of leaves.

Soon they got close enough to see the iron pots and pans hanging from the outer posts of the shack. Large boulders were stacked just outside the front to make a windbreak. It appeared to be a camp and not a dwelling.

Closer they approached until they began to see the fire in the shack and the feet of a man not far from the flames.

John stopped and called out, "Hello to camp."

The voice of an elderly man replied loud and clear, "Come on in. Get your eyes full of this smoke."

Aerenthia gave John a strange look and he replied. "There is no cross wind to move the smoke out."

The smoke of the fire burled over the outer edges of the shack roof. John and Aerenthia walked in and sat on stumps across from their host with their heads lowered below the smoke.

That far from the black mountain, the sun did shine, though many hours after it had risen in

Anglamora. The morning in the canyon was a dim morning light, just enough to see the ground until late in the day.

Finally, a slight breeze blessed them by moving the smoke out of the lean two and they were able to see the man for the first time.

He was leaned back in a log frame chair with his hands resting on his chest. His beard and hair were short and grey. He wore overalls and work boots which confused John Porter.

"You're from Moderna I assume?" John asked.

The man replied. "I was... Now, I am from here. It took me many years to convince the bears to let me stay, but we finally come to an agreement."

John asked. "You talk to them do you?"

The Timekeeper laughed and said, "All things in nature talk if you're willing to listen. Once you learn it, I do not recommend telling others. That is unless you're uncertain if you want them to stay or not."

Aerenthia was looking to the back of the shack behind the man. There was a stick frame bed with many blankets on it and a few clothes hanged from a log rafter overhead.

The back wall and ceiling were lined with clocks and pocket watches hanged down like an endless windchime.

The Timekeeper asked. "What is the reason I am blessed with a visit from the Grim Reaper and Anglamora's most beloved star?"

It was obvious John Porter was the Grim, given the scythe he carried. Aerenthia could not believe he knew who she was.

She asked. "How is it you know who I am when I have never seen you before now?"

The man had a grin on his face and waited for a moment before he replied.

"Everyone within this realm of the ice wall knows who you are. We know because Evelyn Murray told us who you are."

John asked. "You knew Evelyn?"

He replied. "Of course I did. That's why you're here. To find out how for her, time doesn't count. You want to learn how to bend time?"

Aerenthia replied. "Correct... Well, mostly. We do not want to bend time. We do want to know how Evelyn can?"

The man smiled and said, "It is the question we all want the answer to. I asked her many long years ago and she would not say. Though she left me a clue that I will pass to you."

John was fidgeting with his hands and slightly twisting his boot on the ground. The Timekeeper picked up a stick he had leaned against his chair. One end of it was burned as he used it for a poker in the fire. He hit John on the side of the leg with the stick.

"Quit fidgeting and be still!" The man said as he leaned the stick back against his chair.

John had a slight angry look as he asked. "Was that necessary?"

"Yes it was... You can't listen or learn anything while you're fidgeting. Be still and listen." The Timekeeper said as he leaned the stick back against him.

John asked. "What was the clue?"

The man got up and took down and pocket watch from the ceiling and passed it to John.

John opened the watch and saw the second hand was bouncing in one spot unable to move forward.

"This one doesn't work." John said to him.

The Timekeeper replied. "Yes it does."

John looked it over again to make sure the second hand was still in the same spot.

"No... This is stuck. It doesn't work." John said with a more direct tone.

The Timekeeper sat down, and John kept fidgeting with the watch and moving in his seat. He quickly felt the sting of the stick against his leg again.

John looked at the man with a disgusted look. The Timekeeper had a grin on his face.

Aerenthia said to him, "Was that really necessary?"

The Timekeeper replied. "Well yes. Neither one of you are listening. Now sit still, be quiet for a minute and listen."

They did what was asked and soon the crackling of the fire was replaced with the ticking of the clocks behind the Timekeeper.

Aerenthia was first to notice. She looked at John and said, "The clocks."

John looked at the clocks and noticed the second hand on all of them were not moving forward but were bouncing.

"None of them work," John said to him.

He replied. "They all work just fine. They just don't work for you two."

John asked. "How is that possible?"

The Timekeeper replied. "You are the Grim and a star. Time is irrelevant to both of you. Therefore, you cannot see it. To you, time is a theory that does not exist. If you become mortal again, it will."

John and Aerenthia sat very still with their heads down and in deep thought.

"How does that relate to Evelyn being able to stop time?" John asked.

The Timekeeper replied. "I don't know that she ever could completely stop time. I think she moved through time at such a speed it seemed to stop. It is my own theory that she could create a loop in time. If so, she was both mortal and immortal. It would explain why in Anglamora alone, the young never age and the old never die."

John and Aerenthia looked at each other and John slightly shook his head. Aerenthia squinted her eyes at John.

She said in a low voice, "Does that mean she is still alive?"

The Timekeeper asked. "What do you mean by still alive?"

John replied. "She passed away just two days ago. I was the one who was forced to do it."

The Timekeeper leaned forward looking John in the eyes.

"The Grim cannot kill Evelyn Murray. The Grim stops the time we have in the form we have. That is what death is."

Aerenthia asked. "Are you saying she is still alive?"

He replied. "She is the cycle. Without Evelyn Murray, there can be no cycle. She may not be in her old form but make no mistake. She planted the seeds for her return.

"I don't know for sure, but I believe it's how the three seconds are missing. I believe she created loops in time using a second for each. One for Moderna, one for Anglamora and one for her return.

"The only way to know for sure is this. If that watch I gave you works in the hands of a mortal, it will stop again, bouncing for three seconds if Evelyn holds it."

"If that happens, then you will know how it is possible for time not to count for Evelyn Murray. Within her loops, she can travel to any point she wants. She could appear and seemingly disappear."

John said to him, “I have seen her do that.”

He replied. “Many have. Yet, only in Moderna. She uses gates and doors here. I often wonder if she creates loops in such a way that she is born again in a different place or time. Would that explain her longevity? Could that be how she is the oldest of them all? The only way to know is to find the missing three seconds.”

Aerenthia asked. “You said death only stops time in that form... For Evelyn Murray, time does not count. Does that mean she is now in a different form?”

“Yes. I believe that.” The Timekeeper said to her.

John asked with a slight grin. “I have to know... In Moderna are you in fact called Father time?”

The Timekeeper laughed and said, “I am not. In Moderna I am known as simply Jay. Just an old man who knows too much and contains too much useless knowledge.”

Aerenthia grinned and said, “Oh I doubt that. I suspect the people of Moderna think more of you.”

“I doubt it... If he whacks their legs like he did mine, I doubt he has any friends.” John said as he smiled at Aerenthia and the Timekeeper.

His remark was met by a laugh from the other two and the Timekeeper said to him, “Well, be still and listen.”

After a short laugh from the three of them, a more serious quiet tone took over. John and Aerenthia were leaned forward with their elbows on their knees as they thought about it all.

The Timekeeper seemed to be reading their minds.

"I can tell you, if a deal was made, she cannot return in her form unless the other party does not hold to their end of it. The Mediator will enforce the deal."

Aerenthia quickly replied. "Yes I know."

John asked. "How do we find the missing three seconds?"

The Timekeeper replied. "She will have told you if she wanted you to know. It will be in your memories. It will be a memory you don't even know you have."

Aerenthia asked. "How could we possibly remember something we don't know we have a memory of?"

"You will have to enter a deep sleep. Then separate your mind and body so the dream becomes a memory. To do this you will need help. You will have to find the Dream Weaver. In Moderna he is called the Sandman." The Timekeeper said with a serious tone.

John said to him, "How will any of this help us defeat Luciftias?"

The Timekeeper leaned back in his chair and said, "Time is power. The powers of this world are times and nothing more. You will need a powerful time to defeat him."

John asked. "So I have been told. Now, how do we find the Dream Weaver?"

"You don't find him. You ask for him to bring you a dream. He will find you. With that said, it is about time I put out feed for the bears. It's part of our bargain you see."

John and Aerenthia stood up and Aerenthia said to the man, "Thank you for your knowledge and time."

John nodded and said, "Yes thanks for your time."

The Timekeeper stood up, stretched and said to them, "There was no time involved. The watches and clocks do not work for me either."

John closed his eyes for a moment as he stood still. When he opened them, he gave the man a strange look.

John said, "You have no candle."

The Timekeeper smiled and said, "Not anymore."

The man walked to the side of the lean two and opened a wooden barrel where he took out a pale of grain. He stopped for a moment as if he were listening to something in a far distance.

He said to John and Aerenthia, "Two things my new friends... Evelyn Murray is the cycle and for her time doesn't count. Eventually, you two will figure it out."

CHAPTER 2

While John and Aerenthia were leaving the box canyon, Lundar, Theodess, Tanamit and Badru were entering into Danann.

The snowline separated the realms of Anglamora and Danann at the top of the eastern mountain. Max's old trail was loose rock and black stones. The other side of the same mountain was snow covered.

In the far east from their position, the small group could see smoke rising from where the capitol city of Muldibar would be located.

Lundar said to his company of men, "Smoke rises from Muldibar. What madness has come to this place?"

Badru said to him, "We must hurry."

The men made haste down the mountainside toward the bottom and in the direction of the smoke.

In Anglamora, Katie Carpenter was inside the hut looking at the map on the inside of the box lid. She circled Danann with her finger.

"So, this is the location you have chosen for the last great war of our time," she said to herself.

Katie's moment alone was interrupted by a knock on the door. She opened it to see the

Undertaker standing beside Luke and Sanwren. She could see by their black armor, they were ready for her command.

The Undertaker asked. “Any news?”

“Nothing yet... Though my stomach says we will know soon enough” Katie replied.

Luke looked around and asked. “Where is John Porter and Aerenthia?”

Katie replied. “They have gone to see the Timekeeper.”

The Undertaker said to her, “That’s a fool’s errand. Mother is gone. Trying to find the missing three seconds won’t change anything.”

The three men stepped inside and Katie shut the door.

“It is not a fool’s errand Mark... Your mother was part of a cycle John will start anew.” Katie said to him.

Luke gave his view of things. “I am surprised Anglamora’s army isn’t assembled. I thought we were going to enter the forbidden lands and whip somebody’s ass.”

Katie grinned and said, “I do not believe the war will happen in that place... I believe Danann will be the target of Luciftias. We must prepare for an invasion from the east.”

The Undertaker said to her, “King Darr would never attack Anglamora.”

Katie replied. “We are soon to find out. Lundar took a small company of men and one reaper with him to see King Darr. Soon, we will know if he is friend or foe."

Outside of Lundar, Theodess, Tanamit and Badru, twenty of Lundar's men had come with them.

As they approached Muldibar they could hear the screaming and yelling of men and women in a great struggle.

Lundar said to his company, "We must go directly to King Darr before we engage in any battles we can avoid... Remember, this is no longer our homeland."

Lundar was in good fortune as the white stone castle was on the west side of the city. The King's castle of Danann only covered a half-acre in size. It was built around the main tower in the center where the philosopher's stone rested on a pedestal at the top chamber.

When Lundar and his men approached, one of the King's guards yelled out.

"They have flanked us! They're coming from the west!"

Lundar quickly yelled back, "I am King Lundar of the eastern shore of Danann. I have returned."

Lundar and his company stood still with their hands up in the air, as they were quickly surrounded by many guards.

The guards of Danann were all dressed in white leather armor. In one hand they carried shields and spears in the other. The bowmen were on the roof.

A guardsman with long blonde hair and blue eyes walked up to Lundar and looked him over.

"I was a friend of King Lundar for an age. I was his friend before he abandoned Danann." The guard said to him.

"Surely, the Captain of the King's guards would know I did not abandon my homeland and people... My friend, Aziel, it was Lady Fate who sent us to Boagar forest where we remained." Lundar pleaded.

Aziel replied. "King Darr will know if you speak the truth."

Lundar looked past Aziel to the white stone city that was in turmoil and burning in the east.

"What madness has come this place?" Lundar asked.

Aziel replied. "We do not know. It came like a thief in shadow. It came with rumors, and lewdness. Then conspiracies began to take hold to take down our beloved King. It began with fights and murders. Now Danann is split and the enemy, that is our own people are advancing daily."

"Tanamit... You and your men follow Aziel's command and help where you can. Theodess, Badru and I will go talk to King Darr."

Aziel said to Lundar. "You must leave your weapons at the door until we know if you are friend or foe."

The weapons were handed over. As they walked around the castle to the door, many of the guardsmen, stared at Badru.

At the door, Aziel said to Badru, "You have never been here or met our great king. He will look like a boy to you. Make no mistake my painted friend, you are no match for him."

Aziel opened the door and held his hand out for the three of them to walk in. Once they stepped inside, he said to them, "He is at the top."

Aziel shut the door and stayed outside. Badru asked Theodess and Lundar.

"He is not a good guardsman. Should he think we are the enemy why would he leave us alone with the King?"

Theodess replied. "You are a big man Badru and we are all experienced warriors. The three of us would not last half a minute in battle against King Darr without our weapons. Maybe only a minute with them."

The inside of the castle was the same white stones as the outside, yet much cleaner. There were languages and drawings carved in the stones of the inside as well. The floor of the main entrance room was a giant compass made of black stones, outlined by the white stones. Around the compass was also a map of Danann and the eastern shore and ice wall.

Against the far wall was a set of stairs that spiraled up toward the top. The three men began their journey up the stairs with no wasted time. King Darr's council was of great urgency.

At the top of the stairs there was a round doorway with no door attached. Before entering, Lundar announced himself.

"I am Lundar… King of the eastern shore. Friend of Danann, friend of King Darr and servant of justice."

A slow light raspy voice answered him, "Enter my friend, Lundar."

From the doorway they could see the floor of this room was a complete map of all three realms withing the ice wall. The wings of giant birds covered most of the walls. Each wing appeared to be nearly ten feet in length.

The men stepped inside the room at the top of the tower and Badru saw King Darr for the first time.

He appeared to be a twelve- to fourteen-year-old skinny boy with brown hair. He was clothed with a mere leather cloth wrapped around his waist. His upper body, legs and bare feet were completely exposed.

Between them was a black pedestal with the foot of a worhawk mounted upside down so the talons held the philosopher's stone.

Lundar and Theodess bowed their heads to King Darr who was focused on Badru.

"My good King, we come to seek your council," Lundar said to him.

King Darr only nodded to the two of them before he walked to stand next to Badru. King Darr rubbed his index finger on Badru's arm.

"I have never seen a painted man before." King Darr said to Badru.

Badru replied. "I am not painted. I am black. In my homeland, most of us are."

King Darr replied. "You have come for council... Have you also come to fight against the evil that has swept this land?"

Badru answered. "I am a reaper of darkness and shadow, no matter where it may appear. If it is evil that has swept your land, I am an enemy of it."

King Darr walked to the philosopher's stone as Badru looked at his other two companions with a concerned look.

King Darr said to Badru. "If we both stand against the same evil, it must mean we were made by the same creator. Therefore, it must be that we are brothers you and I."

Darr turned to Lundar and Theodess giving them a comforted look before he looked to one of the tall rectangular openings of the outer wall.

"Fate cast you from your homeland and you returned from the west. To the west is where it will end." King Darr suggested to Lundar.

Lundar replied. "How is it you know Lady Fate cast us out?"

Darr answered him. "It was Fate and Destiny who said it must be done. You were to become Anglamorians before your return. Now, the alliance will be formed."

Theodess said to him, "We could have formed the alliance without spending such time in Boagar forest."

"No... It happened as it was supposed to my good man, the night watchman." Darr said with a smile.

Lundar asked. "How do you know all these things? We never once consulted with Anglamora before. How can you know about Theodess seeing in the dark?"

King Darr replied. "Because I was told his destiny, and it is a great destiny. What you have failed to learn, I have not.

"Long before the old one marched across the ice, this day was already prepared for us. It is the cycle of all things and ever repeating. We all must face the darkness and we all must choose a side."

Badru said to King Darr. "If this day was already prepared for us, then the outcome is already prepared."

King Darr walked to the side of the room and took a white spear out of a rack. He stood it beside himself as he faced Badru.

"This day is prepared for us as opportunity to make decisions. No one decides for us. Not even the creator. Opportunities are given and it is up to us to choose wisely." King Darr replied.

Lundar said to Darr, "The old one, Evelyn Murray is dead. A deal was made to protect Anglamora from a great evil. I fear that decision has led that same evil here."

King Darr went to look closely at the philosopher's stone. It was a blue crystal of abnormal shape as it was unrefined or carved since it was brought out of the ground.

King Darr said to them, "I do not need this stone to know Evelyn Murray is not dead. She is resting and giving that evil you speak of an opportunity. Though she cannot rise in the form she was, she is still alive."

The three men glanced at each other. King Darr knew what was on their mind.

He answered their unspoken question. "She will not join us. She will not return here. Here in Danann we must defeat this evil alone."

Badru said to him, "Not alone."

King Darr smiled at Badru and said, "Danann is in your debt."

King Darr walked to the opening in the wall and looked out across the white city. A silence fell in the room and the yells and screams of the city turmoil could be heard.

Darr said to them, "They painted their armor red... Those who have chosen the darkness. They only seek to destroy all good things, unwillingly to admit, their own actions are causing their pain.

"The red army outnumber us ten to one. So many have fallen to the temptations of shadow. For all my years, I have carried peace in my heart. Now I carry anger. Should they see the white tower fall to darkness, they would also seek to cast a dark shadow on Anglamora. It must be defeated here in Danann."

King Darr turned around to look at the men. Badru had his hands cupped around the glowing crystal pendant. Badru's lips moved in a quiet whisper none of the others could hear.

In Anglamora, the pendants of the reapers began to glow. They too had their eyes closed and lips moving. The Undertaker, Luke and Sanwren stood up. Katie took up the white staff.

A moment later the glow faded, and the door of the hut opened. Zethra and Osmo stepped inside.

"Danann calls for aid," Zethra said to them.

It was Katie's decision to make as leader of the Anglamorians.

She looked at Osmo and said, "I know you must feel some loyalty to your former homeland. If I told you not to go, and Danann fell, it would be my fault. If I tell you to go and Anglamora falls, it is also my fault."

The Undertaker said to her, "I will take the children and those who choose not to fight into my realm."

Luke continued where the Undertaker left. "Anglamora is only a place in our hearts. It can be a place anywhere we choose. This fight against the great evils of this world belongs to us all."

"And we must defeat it no matter where it rises." Osmo said to Katie.

Katie replied. "So be it… Osmo, assemble your men for war. The reapers and I will stay together here in Anglamora. It must never again be uninhabited. Osmo will lead our army in this fight."

Luke said with a direct tone. "I belong to no army. Osmo is a great man, but I think Sanwren and I should go ahead while the army is assembled."

Sanwren flexed his chest causing his leather armor to squeak as it stretched. He nodded at Luke who was waiting for an answer.

Osmo said to them, "We are on the same side. Your choice to go alone is yours. I only fear for your safety."

Zethra said to them, "King Darr is in the white tower of the castle. You will know when you see it. Badru, Lundar and Theodess are with him. They are soon to come under attack."

Osmo said to Luke and Sanwren, "Take a bow and many arrows. King Darr will know you are a friend if you come as a friend. Provide cover where you can. When we arrive on the western slope, we charge together."

Zethra said to Luke and Sanwren, "Badru said the enemy army painted their armor red."

CHAPTER 3

Late day fell in Danann and the red army spread around the eastern part of the white city. The army loyal to King Darr were all in white armor and gathered around the white tower. They were numbered at only one thousand.

One thousand who were ready to engage in open war against nearly ten thousand of their former friends and fellow guards.

King Darr was looking out of the rectangular hole toward the east. His boyish appearance would not seem like much of an overwatch to modern man, but it meant everything to those standing below.

King Darr said in his low raspy voice as he watched the smoke rise in the east and getting closer.

"A mind sickened with a terrible thought one desires to be a reality is the greatest threat to the world."

King Darr turned around to face the three men in the room as he asked Badru, "Tell me, did you ask for help or a way out?"

Badru replied. "I informed the other reapers that a darkness lives in Danann we must defeat."

King Darr said to him, “We cannot defeat it standing up here. We must always face the evil things and destroy it where it rises.”

King Darr walked to the side of the chamber and took up a belt with and dagger. There was a leather pouch on one side of the belt and the dagger on the other.

King Darr put the lemon size philosopher’s stone in the pouch and took up his white spear once more.

Theodess asked. “Will you not wear armor my King?”

King Darr replied. “I am always armored… Now, follow me as we enter this war.”

He led them down the spiral stairs to the front door of the small castle. Darr and the three men with him walked to the front of the line of white armored men.

Aziel released Tanamit and his men from watch and returned their weapons to them. Then he went to join Darr and returned the weapons to Lundar and Theodess.

Aziel said to Darr. “Should this be the last of our days, I am honored to fight and die by your side.”

All who were close enough to hear looked at Aziel and King Darr.

Darr replied. “Should this be the last of these evil days, I am honored to defeat them by yours.”

The words of Darr, keeper of the philosopher's stone inspired the white army of Danann.

Tanamit and his men joined Lundar and Theodess.

"Tanamit, ready your men with their bows. Do not wait for my command. When the first red armored man appears, let the arrows fly."

Tanamit nodded and spread his men ten feet apart along the front of the line. Afterwards, he walked out front and turned to face the gathered army and his bowmen.

"You are not under my command now. You are under your own. If this be our last fight together, we fight under the command of self-conviction of right and wrong. We fight as free men against the great evils of this world."

Tanamit turned around to face the east. The sounds of screams and terror grew louder. Many of Danann's citizens were running toward the white army for protection.

The remnants of the citizen population gathered inside and close to the castle behind the white army. Tanamit took off with his limp as he walked toward the east.

A sadness fell on the face of Lundar and Theodess. Lundar took a deep breath as he prepared to yell out but was stopped by King Darr.

Darr had his hand on Lundar's chest. Theodess and Lundar looked at Darr with great confusion.

King Darr said to them as he threw his crown of worhawk talons on the ground.

"Each of us must face evil in a different way. Tanamit chooses to face it alone. It is not ours to stop him."

Darr and his standing army watched as Tanamit slowly disappeared in the smoke next to the white stone buildings in the city.

"When darkness falls upon us, it will be you who leads us my friend Theodess." King Darr said to him.

Darr turned to Aziel and nodded. Aziel gave the call. "Form the ready line."

The white army marched forward beyond the bowmen and locked their shields together overlapping one another. They lowered their spears in their right hands.

The second row lowered spears in their left hands and let them rest on the shields of those in front. King Darr was the only one not standing in a row. He was out front of them all with his spear in both hands, down at his side.

Darr and his men did not have to wait long before the red army appeared through the smoke of the burning city.

The Bowmen standing behind the white army wasted no time and waited for no command. The distance was far for an arrow at nearly one hundred yards across the courtyard.

As the red army approached the arrows arched high and began to hit the men at the third and fourth row.

One of the bowmen yelled out, "Don't stop until we are out of arrows. Let them all fly!"

The red army was at a slight disadvantage. Due to the buildings and smoke behind them, they could not form together at once. King Darr saw this and ordered his army to charge.

The white army clashed against the red shields and armor at the smoke line. They were equal in number at this point. The men of the red army coming out of the city into the battle were displaced, confused and undisciplined.

Even as the red army seemed to fall row by row, they were ten thousand strong and slowly gathering together.

King Darr stood alone moving with lightning speed. With spear and dagger in hand he had an open circle made around himself in a sea of red.

The bowmen had moved forward and were firing into the smoke past the battle. They knew those coming from the city would not be able to see the arrows through the smoke and fire.

The war was underway in Danann. At the same time all was quiet in Anglamora. Anglamora's army had gone to the east and only a few residents remained. Mountain Max was sitting by the firepit outside of Evelyn's hut. Katie and the reapers were inside.

Night had returned to Anglamora and this time there were no fires on the slopes around the stream. Inside the hut, Katie sat in Evelyn's chair and the reapers sat on the benches and hearth of the fireplace.

"I wish Zethra had stayed," Katie said to the others.

Kenji replied. "She will never leave Osmo's side."

Katie said to them. "I believe we are being deceived. I have given this great thought. The Tuatha De' Danann were never part of this fight. I can't help but think because they are so far to the east, Luciftias will come from the west."

Mateo said to her, "Locklure is neutral. He cannot come from the west."

Katie lowered her eyes in deep thought. She was not convinced by Locklure's neutrality.

Karma, Fate and Destiny were still on top of the black mountain in Locklure and they did not go unnoticed. King Eshnar joined them and boldly stated.

"Evelyn Murray made the rules in Anglamora. I make the rules in Locklure. I know all things that are here. Even as they conspire on top of this mountain."

"You are wise friend, Eshnar... King of Locklure." Destiny said to him.

Fate followed. "Conspire you say... Surely not us."

Eshnar grinned and said, “It is what you do. It is for us to find out and learn. That is why I am here now. Why have you gathered on this mountain? What is beyond the ice you await?”

Karma answered. “We cannot tell you what is beyond the ice.”

“We can say, we are waiting for something that is coming from beyond the ice. You must prepare for it King Eshnar.” Destiny told him.

King Eshnar replied. “According to Evelyn Murray, the only thing past the ice is Adierach. It is too far for them to cross it.”

Fate said to him, “She crossed it.”

Eshnar’s eyes grew wide. Without saying another word, he turned and went back the way he had come. Once again the three deities stood alone.

When Eshnar had gone, Destiny asked. “Who will be the karma of the other? Will it be Locklure who is Adierach’s karma or Adierach who comes for justice?”

Karma looked toward the distant ice wall but did not reply.

King Eshnar met with a druid halfway down the mountain.

The king demanded. “Find John Porter and Aerenthia. If you cannot find them in one day’s time, blow the horn to gather.”

Aerenthia and John at that time were approaching the firepit in Anglamora where Max was standing.

Mountain Max said to them, “It is very quiet here in Anglamora now. It has not been this quiet in a very long time.”

John asked. “What is going on?”

Max replied. “Anglamora’s army is marching east to join with Danann. The children are at the tomb of the Undertaker in Erissa’s care.

“Only a few mystics stayed behind in their homes. Katie and some of the reapers are inside the hut.”

“Chaos has woken in Danann. Now Anglamora is unprotected.” Aerenthia said to Max.

Max replied. “Not unprotected... We are here.”

Aerenthia looked at John who knew what she was thinking.

John said to her, “Yes, return to the sky and see what you can see.”

Aerenthia began to glow and rise as she slowly turned into an orb and descended into the night sky.

John and Max were looking up at the sky when the Undertaker said from behind them, “It is a sight when she does that.”

The two men turned to face Mark and gave him a nod.

John asked. “How is Erissa?”

Mark replied. “Her strength is returning. The children I believe are blessing to her. Now she isn’t sitting alone.”

Max asked. "Will you join the war in the east or stay and see Anglamora safe?"

Mark replied. "Anglamora is safe… A deal was made, and it will be kept. I will go east and join the others."

Max asked John. "What about you?"

"I am the Grim. I cannot kill men at will. I can only take them when their candles have lost the flame."

Max grinned and said, "Hide the scythe. Let them touch you."

John replied. "I cannot. I cannot influence them to unknowingly choose death."

Mark said to John, "You don't have to. If you and I show up in Danann, Luciftias will show up as well. He is too arrogant not to."

The door of the hut opened, and Katie stepped out carrying the white staff. The three men gave her a nod of respect.

John said to her, "Surely Anglamora is safe with you here while we are going east to Danann."

Katie replied. "I wish you would go west to Locklure. I have a strange feeling something is going on there."

"If so, Eshnar would have sent a rider. The war is to the east." John told her.

Mark said to her, "Send a reaper. If there is a problem in Locklure, they can report back to all the other reapers. Even as far away as Danann."

Katie replied. "Okay. I will do that."

“Aerenthia is in the sky seeing what she can right now.” John said to her.

Max said to them. “I will go with the reaper to see King Eshnar. If anything stirs in Locklure, he will know.”

Katie said to them. “Here in the last war of our time, we are without Evelyn Murray. Should the evil of Danann spread, all will be undone. Our army joins a King I do not know because of an enemy we share.

“All these powers we have bestowed upon us. A star from heaven to watch over us, the white staff of eternal light, a gate keeper, Grim and Undertaker. Yet we are the ones under attack. It is as it has always been. The good things of this world under the ever-relentless attack of darkness. Should we lose this war, the dream is over, and the cycle of all things undone.”

CHAPTER 4

Max and the reaper Mateo went west toward Locklure. John Porter faded to a plume of black smoke and the Undertaker disappeared.

Katie Carpenter stood alone at the firepit until the morning twilight came. She had a wooden nickel in her hand she stared at for some time.

Destiny appeared across the fire from Katie and said, “I have always admired your wooden nickels.”

“A hug is priceless Destiny.” Katie replied.

Destiny continued. “There is great power within those nickels… Power to bring the dead back to life across the astral plane. Power to cause a Grim to begin a new cycle.”

Katie asked. “You want me to give one to John Porter?”

“No… I want you to give one to Evelyn Murray.” Destiny replied.

Katie squinted her eyes at Destiny as she was very confused. Destiny only grinned in return.

While Katie was entertaining Destiny, John and the Undertaker appeared on the western slope of Danann alongside Sanwren and Luke.

The four of them stayed in the snow and forest of the mountainside as they tried to work their way around to the south side of the city.

Once they got close enough, Luke and Sanwren began firing arrows toward the red army. Neither of them were very accurate, but the enemy were so large in number it didn't matter.

The Undertaker had his large double bit axe in front of him as he watched with a disgusted look.

"They will not be able to defeat the red army." John said them.

The Undertaker replied. "Not as it stands. If they can survive the night, Osmo will be here at daylight."

Luke said to the rest. "I'm no good with this damn bow. I rather join the fight down there."

Sanwren thumped his chest in agreement.

John said to them, "There is nothing I can do here."

The Undertaker replied. "Stay with us. We have to draw Luciftias out."

The full moon of the night sky in Danann along with the fires burning in the city, gave enough light for the fight to continue.

King Darr and his army were slowly falling back toward the white castle as they tried to fight off an ever growing number of their enemy.

John Porter appeared among the spears between the armies as he stood looking at King

Darr. His scythe glowed red and black smoke rose from his feet.

Men from both armies backed away from him, leaving him in an open circle between the front lines.

John spoke in the mind of King Darr, “I will be bringing in three men dressed in black from the south. Order your men not to attack them.”

King Darr nodded and whispered to Aziel who was at his side. Aziel gave John a quick look before he took off running toward the south end of the line.

From behind John a man from the red army said, “I do not fear death.”

Upon his words, a spear went through John, but it was as if it went through smoke instead of a man. John turned around, as a ghostly figure and faced the man. The spear was still through him. John used the scythe and gently touched the spear burning it in half. The back half hit the ground behind John who had a smile on his face.

The men close by from both armies watched in awe.

“If you have no fear as you say, touch me.” John said to the man.

The man laughed and said, “I do not believe in candles and the Grim. I determine my own life and death.”

The man walked up to John and held up one finger from a closed fist and tried to poke John in the chest. However, upon touching him, the man fell dead instantly.

The red army formed a larger circle around John who said to them, “Cross the burning line and you will die.”

Upon his words, John changed to black smoke and the glowing scythe streaked down the line between the armies burning the spears in half. As the scythe returned, it left a burning line of fire on the ground between the armies.

John appeared beside King Darr and said in a low voice, “It won’t kill them. But it will give you time to pull your men back and regroup.”

King Darr nodded and John disappeared. King Darr ordered his army back to the white castle. The white army formed three lines of men across the front of the castle. Darr and Theodess went up the white tower to Darr’s chambers.

Lundar ordered the bowmen to take what arrows they had left and position themselves on the roof top. At that same time, John returned with Aziel, the Undertaker, Luke and Sanwren.

Luke and Sanwren offered their bows to Lundar for someone more qualified to use. The red army backed up beyond the distance white arrows could fly.

King Darr looked down upon the two armies with the full moon above him. Theodess stood silent in the center of the room. Minutes passed and King Darr finally spoke to Theodess.

"I have been here so long and been King Darr for so long I have forgotten my first name. My friend, old Evelyn crossed the ice and long before I crossed the sea. I too was from one of the three continents of the third realm.

"After finding the philosopher's stone, I traveled here and killed the worhawks that plagued this land... All but one I raised from a chick who is now a dear friend I call Old Toby... Do you remember Theodess?"

Theodess said in a somber tone. "I do."

King Darr continued. "In all my long years I wondered when the darkness of the third realm would seek us out for destruction. I hoped we would be so steadfast in our morality we would never fall. Tell me, my friend Theodess, what are your thoughts?"

Theodess replied. "I dare not say what my true thoughts are."

King Darr turned around to face Theodess before he said, "Here at the end of all things, the truth is all we have. Do not be afraid to speak it."

Theodess lowered his head for a moment as he gathered his thoughts before speaking.

"My great King and friend, I do not believe the darkness and malice of the third realm traveled so far for you alone. It came for the old one, Evelyn Murray. Now that she is dead, Danann is a distraction."

King Darr grew a very curious look and moved slow and methodically to stand in front of Theodess before he asked.

"To you was given the power to see in the dark. Tell me what my eyes cannot see. Tell me what I may or may not be failing to understand. Why do you say we are a distraction?"

Theodess swallowed hard and said, "We are only fighting among ourselves here. There are no physical beings here from the third realm. We are fighting ideologies while I believe the physical army is following Evelyn's path across the ice."

"Adierach." King Darr said in a low voice.

"Aye." Theodess replied.

King Darr took up the small stone from the talons of the worhawk foot and gripped it tight as he closed his eyes. After a moment, he looked to Theodess.

"Maybe it is you Theodess, guardian of the night who should be king. Anglamora's army marches east to our aid leaving Locklure to stand alone... Bring me the painted reaper."

Theodess gave a nod and turned to leave the room. King Darr returned to look out of the rectangular window.

Outside of the white castle John Porter, the Undertaker, Aziel, Lundar, Sanwren and Luke were standing together. The remaining survivors and minor wounded of the white army watched them as if they were expecting a miracle.

The conversation of those men was interrupted by the loud raspy voice of Theodess who was asking for Badru to come forward. Without hesitation, the reaper answered the call and went to Theodess who was seen whispering to him.

Badru went inside the castle and Theodess joined the leadership of the white army.

"What of King Darr?" Asked Aziel.

Theodess replied. "We believe it is possible Danann is a distraction. The physical army of Luciftias and Shadow will come from the west. It will come from Locklure. It is possible we have left the druids to their doom."

A brief silence fell among them as they let their minds wonder. John Porter eventually broke the silence.

"I can be there and back near instantly. I will go see King Eshnar."

The Undertaker put his hand on John's chest and said, "No. The plan is to stay here and draw Luciftias out. Then kill him."

Lundar said to John. "He is right my friend. What would it matter if you saw ruin in Locklure? You cannot kill the enemy at will. We cannot get there with the red army on our heels."

Luke said to them. "Osmo and company will be here by first light. We just have to hold on till then."

John quickly said, "They will eventually figure out that burning line is meaningless."

Lundar explained. “Even when Osmo gets here he is only accompanied by ten thousand. There are at least eight thousand left of the red army. Maybe fifteen hundred of the white army. We will win, yes but what will be left? How do we face another army with so few?”

Theodess said to all of them as he kept his eyes on John.

“We are faced against a terrible darkness. I cannot see the dark because I have seen a terrible light. We need Shadow’s karma… What darkness could stand against her?”

His words inspired all who could hear him. John asked. “Who do we ask her to save, us or Locklure?”

The Undertaker replied. “Whoever most needs her to be a light in their darkness.”

As they spoke, one of the men from the white army stood up and said to others around him.

“I have to hit the bushes. The anticipation and silence has my stomach in knots.”

The other men nodded as they understood, and many felt the same way. The soldier walked to a grove of small evergreens growing at the slope of the western mountain.

Just as he got in a position out of view of the others, when he began to loosen his armor, Luciftias appeared behind him. The cloaked pale man gently tapped the soldier with his staff.

For only a second, the soldier's eyes turned black as he stood stiff as a board. Luciftias disappeared and the soldier shook his head as if he were waking himself up.

At the top of the castle in King Darr's chamber, Badru was holding his pendant and mumbling.

King Darr stood silently watching until Badru opened his eyes ready to report.

"A fellow reaper has reached Locklure and says the three deity's are standing on top of the lonely black mountain looking north. Karma, Destiny and Fate seem to be waiting for something to come across the ice.

"Katie Carpenter suspects an attack from the west. None have seen Lady Starlight. We are all on our own."

The seriousness of the situation could be seen in King Darr's face.

Badru said to him, "I wish I could report better news."

King Darr patted Badru on the arm and nodded, yet remained silent as no words were needed.

Just as Badru was about to leave the chamber, King Darr said to him, "Do not tell the others what you have told me."

King Darr returned to the opening to see faint twilight in the eastern sky and John Porter standing among the red army.

The Grim Reaper was putting on a show as he stood silent with his eyes hidden by his full brim hat and fire burning at his feet.

This time the soldiers of the red army were standing silent and not challenging his authority.

John said to them. "I am the keeper of candles and the harvester of life. Yet I beg each of you to live, to choose life. You have forsaken your own king and fellow man to serve a master you have not seen. All this, just to satisfy your own desires… Still we wish you to live, but live in peace. What say you?"

A big man who was by his demeanor, obviously the leader of the red army replied.

"The days of tradition and old structures of society are over. We will rule ourselves and kill all those who seek to rule over us."

The red army nodded and cheered at the words of their leader. John said to them.

"And if you were to be victorious, you would then begin to kill each other. Chaos is never satisfied. You have until the sun rises to choose surrender or death."

John disappeared and reappeared among his companions of the white army. He said to Aziel.

"Make ready your men. When the sun rises the fire line will fade."

The twilight grew brighter in the morning sky over Danann. The Red army stood in formation as they were preparing a final assault on what was left of the white army.

Aziel had his men lined up with shields locked. All but ten of the bowmen stood in the ready line with swords instead of bows... Only ten still had arrows.

From the window above, King Darr began to whistle a loud single tone whistle. Three times he whistled before he was interrupted by a familiar voice from the western slope.

"Form the ready line!"

Osmo and the Anglamorian army had made it to Danann and were descending from the snowy slope of the western mountain.

The white army of Danann began to cheer. Osmo and Zethra were out front and gaining speed as the army behind them began to form a V.

King Lundar saw that Osmo was not going to stop so he ordered the white army to charge.

King Darr had a small leather pouch on his side which contained the philosopher's stone. With his spear in hand and dagger sheathed beside the pouch, King Darr ran and jumped from the window.

Only those in the red army saw King Darr's jump and only the red army saw the worhawk circle the white castle.

The chest and stomach of the worhawk was a pale grey and its back and wings were coal black. To the witnesses of the red army, it seemed to have a twenty foot wingspan and a beak made of wrought iron.

King Darr landed on the back of the worhawk and flew over the red army. Theodess yelled out to the others, “It’s Old Toby!”

King Darr and Old Toby circled to the north and slowly faded out of sight beyond the northern mountains.

The red army viewed King Darr’s actions as an act of self-preservation and abandonment of his own men.

The Undertaker and John Porter stood side by side in front of the white castle as they watched the two armies clash. Osmo and the Anglamorian army pierced deep into the red army. Their flanks spread wide with the white army on the northern end of the line.

Zethra and Badru were highly trained along with the Anglamorian army trained in swordsmanship by Aerenthia.

The giant Sanwren used his shovel and strength to destroy anyone who close to him. Luke was having a best day of his life.

As enemy soldiers tried to run from Sanwren, Luke said to him from a short distance away.

“There’s enough of them for both of us Sanwren. You take that half and I’ll take this one.”

Sanwren tapped his chest and rushed into a cluster of red soldiers pushing against white shields.

As they watched, the Undertaker said to John.

"I suspect he will show when it looks like we are weak. You must find Aerenthia."

CHAPTER 5

War raged on in Danann. Katie Carpenter made a bold decision to warn Locklure by sending the reaper Akeno to the western mountain. He was to instruct the druid there to blow the horn of ruin.

Not long after Akeno left, King Darr and Old Toby landed in the clearing just out front of Evelyn's hut. The boyish looking king slid down the wing of the worhawk and stood with his spear in hand.

The reaper Kenji pulled his sword. King Darr said to him, "Do not be a fool."

The door of the hut opened, and Katie walked outside with a fellowship of reapers at her side.

King Darr slightly bowed his head as he introduced himself. Katie quickly instructed Kenji to sheath his sword before introducing herself.

"Danann is in debt to Anglamora. As our armies battle a great evil in my homeland, I offer myself to be of service here."

Katie Carpenter said to him. "Shouldn't you be leading your own men?"

King Darr replied. "I can lead them, or I can help them. I seek your wandering star. I seek to keep a safe path for their march west."

Katie squinted her eyes and said, "I have not seen Lady Starlight in several days. I do not know where she is."

King Darr bowed his head before he mounted the worhawk.

He said to her, "I will return to Danann. Should you need me, send word by your reapers."

Katie quickly said to him, "Before you return home, go to the lonely black mountain. Lady Starlight may be among the deities there."

King Darr nodded and took off towards the west. Katie looked at the reapers standing with her and said, "I have heard many tales of King Darr. I'm shocked at his appearance."

Locklure was making battle preparations when the short wide horn of Ruin sounded. Upon hearing it, the druids stopped what they were doing and stood in shock.

As the echo crossed the valley of Anglamora, Katie lowered her head in disappointment. The reapers put their hands together in prayer.

Descending from the eastern mountain on Max's road from Danann, a single soldier from the white army was heading into Anglamora.

It didn't take long on the back of the worhawk for King Darr to land on top of the lonely black mountain in Locklure.

The three deities were shocked to him. As he approached on foot, Destiny was first to address him.

"King Darr of Danann… Keeper of the philosopher's stone. What brings you outside of your realm to this mountain?"

King Darr replied. "Word has reached my ears that you three are looking north as if you are waiting for something to cross the ice wall. I come to see for myself."

Fate said to him, "It is not for you to know."

King Darr grinned before he replied with his slow raspy boyish voice.

"Karma, Destiny and Fate are only a time and philosophy. Make no mistake. I do not answer to you."

Karma said to him. "You are correct. You do not. That does not mean we have to tell you. Nor does that mean we are your enemy."

King Darr slightly bowed his head before he replied.

"You are also correct. I apologize for my defensiveness. A darkness has come to Danann. A darkness I fear that may consume the entirety of this realm if it is not defeated. I seek the wandering star."

Upon his words a faint glow consumed the top of the mountain. Destiny pointed to behind King Darr.

He turned around to see her for the first time. In his eyes, she was like an angel. Just as she was to so many when they first saw her. She was standing barefoot on the black flint with her white gown glowing like a beacon in the dark.

King Darr said to her. "Surely you are as magnificent as the stories told. I am humbled to be in your presence. I am King Darr of Danann."

"I have many names. Evelyn Murray gave me the name Aerenthia. She said it means, from the air she came. The Anglamorians call me Lady Starlight. In my worst of times, I am called Fury. The most treasured name I am called is a friend."

Aerenthia offered a handshake to King Darr. He took her hand and kissed the back of it before he pleaded with her.

"A great evil and darkness has come to Danann. An evil from beyond this realm. The Anglamorians have joined us in battle and the Grim waits to face Luciftias. We will win the war on our own but at the cost of many lives. I ask if you would return with me only for an inspirational purpose? I believe if our enemy could see the light, they would choose to shed the darkness."

Aerenthia replied. "It would be an honor to destroy the darkness in your land or wherever it may rise."

King Darr said to her, "I am in your debt." Aerenthia replied. "A friend once said, to be a light in someone else's darkness is the greatest destiny that can be bestowed upon someone. There will be no debt my new friend."

Aerenthia glanced past King Darr to look at Destiny who was smiling at her and giving a very slight nod of approval.

King Darr bowed his head in respect to the three deities who returned it before he climbed back on the worhawk. He leaned forward to stroke the feathers of the hawk's neck before he spoke to it.

"Old Toby... My dearest friend. Take us home. We have a war to win."

Aerenthia returned to her starlight form as she floated to the sky. King Darr and Old Toby took off toward the east.

Once more, Katie Carpenter and the reapers watched the worhawk fly overhead. This time it flew towards Danann where the battle was still under way.

The Anglamorians and the white army were gaining ground against the red army. The red soldiers were without quality swords and lesser trained.

John Porter and the Undertaker were still watching for the arrival of Luciftias. They were standing in front of the door of the white castle watching the battle take place before them.

John said to Mark. "It pains me to stand here unable to help."

The Undertaker replied. "I understand. Yet we are helping. Just being here is helping and they understand what we are doing."

Before John could say another word, a great thunderous near explosive sound came from the north. It was such a sound that the battle paused but only for a second.

King Darr and Old Toby appeared from the top of the northern mountains. Old Toby was carrying a large boulder in each of his talons preparing to drop them on the red army.

Upon the sight of King Darr's return, cheers could be heard among the fighting and wounded of the white army.

Old Toby began to descend to only a hundred feet from the ground.

Just as the worhawk reached the northern end of the battle, King Darr Jumped from his back with spear and dagger in hand.

At the same time King Darr jumped, the starlight orb came racing over the northern mountain. Both the orb and King Darr landed in the same spot at the same time.

Once more Aerenthia's fall caused a crater in the landscape and a dust cloud that took a full minute to subside. From the dust cloud, the two large boulders hit the ground among a cluster of red soldiers, killing many of them.

When the dust settled both armies could see King Darr and Aerenthia in her armor standing on the bank of the crater. Old Toby was flying back toward the northern mountain for more boulders. Aerenthia drew her swords and King Darr addressed her.

"I ask that on this day, you do not fight for me or for Danann. I ask that no blood be shed in wrath of these evil men."

Aerenthia slowly turned her head to King Darr to seek an answer.

"Then tell me, King Darr. What are we fighting for?"

King Darr took a few steps forward, looked back at Aerenthia and said, "For the one who taught you to be a light in this darkness... Today we fight this evil for Evelyn Murray."

King Darr immediately rushed down the fresh dirt bank toward the enemy and Aerenthia wasted no time in joining him.

King Darr threw his spear at the first of the soldiers he reached, and it went through two, pinning them together. When he got to them, another soldier tried to attack him.

His small frame and lightning speed made him a hard target to hit with heavy axes by armored men. King Darr moved around the red soldier's axe as if he were water and he was cutting the soldier with each pass.

More soldiers came and King Darr grabbed his spear just behind the blade and thrust is forward out of the two soldiers and barely into the stomach of another. King Darr held the back end of the shaft as four mor soldiers gathered around him.

The small king used the shaft of the spear to block swings from the axes and stabbed legs that tried to kick him. He remained mostly under the shaft but moved it in every direction to his advantage. The man at the other end held tight so it would not penetrate any deeper. He was the last to fall when King Darr severed his head with his dagger.

His process and strategy repeated over and over again. Aerenthia stayed close by him and mostly reserved to keep an eye on King Darr. Once she felt confident in his abilities, she did not hold anything back.

She worked her way through the enemy until she was standing next to King Darr. From that point on, she used her power to cast strobes of white light, blinding those charging forward. Although they were blind, they were shown no mercy from Aerenthia and King Darr.

Those two alone were slowly destroying the northern end of the red army. Theodess and the Anglamorians were cleaning up the south end and center of the enemy line. Old Toby continued to drop boulders on clusters of red dressed soldiers.

The few hundred remaining of the white army of Danann lead by Aziel, were cutting through the center/left of the line. Defeat for the red army was certain.

Realizing their defeat, the last five hundred and twenty one red army soldiers surrendered. They dropped their axes and bows as they fell to their knees with their hands up, begging for mercy.

Osmo quickly raised his sword in the air and yelled a single word. "Victory!"

To his left, Zethra had sheathed her sword and dagger then raised her hands together in prayer. The free men of Danann cheered but only for a moment. Their cheers did not last as each of them understood the battle was won, but the war would continue.

Eight thousand Anglamorians and white army soldiers lay dead or severely wounded. Over nine thousand of the red army lay dead on the battlefield.

It was not a big area. The field between the white castle and the city was only a quarter mile and it stretched from mountain to mountain some three miles apart.

King Darr and Aerenthia walked side by side to gather with the others at the center. King Darr addressed Osmo first.

"This battle is over but there is no victory. There are two thousand women and children hiding in the mountain tunnel below the white castle. Their husbands, fathers and friends are gone. No my friend, there is no victory here."

John and the Undertaker watched as King Darr walked towards them with his head down.

The Undertaker said to John, "I was sure Luciftias would show and I was wrong."

John put his hand on the Undertaker's shoulder but didn't say anything.

Luke and Sanwren were sitting on piled bodies as they tended to the several gashes they received.

Luke stopped wrapping his elbow long enough to look at Sanwren and say, "I'm glad you made it."

Sanwren tapped his chest and pointed at Luke as he nodded. Luke looked off to his side and seen Theodess, Lundar, Aziel and many white soldiers gathered around the prisoners.

Osmo and Zethra followed behind King Darr towards the white castle. King Darr stopped beside John and the Undertaker. He turned around and looked to the encircled prisoners. After a moment he let out a soft groan and entered the castle without saying a word to the Grim or the Undertaker.

Badru and Aerenthia were making their way to the white castle behind Osmo and Zethra. By the time Osmo and Zethra made it John and the Undertaker, women began running out of the white castle to check on their loved ones. King Darr kept the children inside the castle with him.

Osmo and Zethra gave a nod to John and Mark but with the sound of the women exiting they did not try to speak.

Badru and Aerenthia hastened their march to the castle. Upon arrival, Aerenthia gave John a hug but wasted no time in informing him of what she saw.

"From the sky I could see Karma, Destiny and Fate on top of the lonely black mountain looking north. I went over the ice wall and I didn't have to go far when my eyes saw what they are waiting for.

"The armies of Adierach are marching across the ice. Legions of men lead by Luciftias are less than two weeks from Locklure."

Osmo said in a low concerned voice, "My God... And we are so few."

Zethra asked. "How many men?"

Aerenthia replied. "Ten legions."

Zethra looked at Osmo because she didn't know how many where in a legion. Osmo told her ten legions would be over fifty thousand men.

Badru asked. "What do we do against such a force?"

Luke answered from behind him. "We kick their ass."

Sanwren nodded at Luke. The Undertaker grinned at Luke and Sanwren. Osmo let his eyes fall to the ground as he slightly shook his head. Zethra gripped tight to Osmo's hand but remained silent.

John said to them. "There are only seven thousand fighting men in Locklure. Here we have maybe two thousand who are healthy enough to fight. I do not think it would be wise to tell the others..."

John stopped and stood still. His eyes grew wide and he quickly looked at the Undertaker and said, "Aunt Katie."

John and the Undertaker instantly disappeared. Immediately after, the pendants of Badru and Zethra began to glow. Both held their pendants and stood silent. A moment later, Zethra opened her eyes and said to the group, "Katie has been wounded by a white soldier."

Without saying a word, Aerenthia returned to the sky and her glow could be seen rushing towards the west.

CHAPTER 6

Katie Carpenter was partially laying on the ground by the firepit. Her head and chest were leaned against the reaper Diego. The other reapers had the white soldier on his knees and surrounded. That is the scene John first saw when he appeared before them.

He leaned down next to Katie and saw the arrow sticking out of her side. It was obvious that it punctured her lungs. She was coughing up pink foamy blood and couldn't speak.

John said to her, "They will pay dearly Aunt Katie... All of them."

He stood up and walked toward the white armored soldier leaving his scythe standing on its own. Behind him, a pecan shell hit the ground followed by the bare feet of the Mediator.

Aerenthia and the Undertaker arrived only seconds behind John and were watching everything unfold. Aerenthia had squatted down and took Katie's hand.

“You cannot save her.” The Mediator said to Aerenthia.

The Undertaker took her hand on the other side and told her he would make sure her crossing was easy.

The Mediator called out to John Porter to stop before he could reach the soldier, but his words fell on deaf ears.

The soldier began to beg and like the words of the Mediator, John was not listening. John Porter, Grim Reaper took hold of the soldier by his neck killing him instantly. Yet his death was not enough.

John intensified his power until both he and the soldier were in flames of a raging blue fire. The soldier quickly turned to ash and a dark shadow could be seen leaving the ashes and it moved across the sky to the northwest.

They all saw the remnants of shadow flee. Aerenthia stood up and began to glow as she was preparing to chase it. She was stopped by the Mediator.

“No Aerenthia! Time for vengeance will come but not now and not by you. The deal was broken. Vengeance will come with someone else.”

John reached his hand out and the scythe responded as it quickly came to him. Upon touching his hand, the blade began to glow red. John Porter pointed the scythe at the Mediator and expressed what everyone there was thinking.

"Bring back Evelyn Murray!" The Grim Reaper said to him as his body trembled in anger.

In Locklure, Mateo reported to King Eshnar and Mountain Max what happened to Katie Carpenter. Max lowered his head, saddened by the news. King Eshnar ordered a druid guard standing close by to blow the horn of wrath. The druid wasted no time in getting on his horse to rush toward the horn towers at the eastern border of Locklure.

At the firepit in Anglamora, the Mediator said to Katie Carpenter, "I will keep you in between until you find her across the plane of time."

Katie nodded and the Mediator took her hand causing her to fall into a state of deep sleep between life and death. As the Mediator lifted her in his arms, he gave his orders to all the rest.

"All of you who have been given great power and all the items of powers must be at the great tomb in the Eternal Cemetery within seven days."

After he spoke, the Mediator disappeared. The Undertaker said to Diego, "Assemble the reapers here."

Karma, Destiny and Fate appeared together outside the door of Evelyn's hut. John took notice and asked, "Are any of you responsible for this?"

Karma replied. "It was my understanding that Luciftias was your enemy. Not us."

Destiny disappeared to reappear standing in front of John. She took his free hand in hers before she spoke to him.

"You have to trust me now, John Porter. Katie understood her destiny. It pleased her. This is a great destiny bestowed upon her."

"You destined her to die here?" John exclaimed in anger.

Destiny replied. "I destined her to save the world. Is it not enough?"

The Undertaker said to her, "It is a great destiny."

John knew they were right. He lowered his eyes and Destiny could see he was sorry for the haste of his anger. She pulled him down so she could hug him around the neck.

John Porter apologized. Destiny whispered to him. "I have only love and a great destiny for you and with it, I have to hurt you sometimes."

Fate said to all of them, "The fate of this world and this cycle now rest with Katie Carpenter and a small wooden object."

Karma continued where Fate left off. "It is the opposite of the evil and darkness you are sworn to fight."

After hearing their words, John looked at Destiny. She could tell he knew what they were talking about. Destiny gave him a wink.

Aerenthia said to the group, "I will return to Danann to help King Darr any way I can. I will keep watch over them as they march into Anglamora."

In Danann, King Darr was being told by Badru about the attack in Anglamora. He was with the small group outside of the castle standing next to Osmo.

After hearing what was said by the Mediator, King Darr turned to face Osmo as he said, “Victory is coming to us.”

Zethra explained to King Darr that she and Badru were ordered to return to Anglamora. He granted their leave and Osmo asked to join them. King Darr shook Osmo’s hand and nodded with a smile.

King Darr looked to Luke and Sanwren, awaiting their request. Luke explained that he and Sanwren would return with the army of Danann, the men they had fought beside.

Luke’s words pleased the boy looking king. Without speaking, King Darr began to walk toward the crowd of guards and prisoners in the middle of the field. Luke and Sanwren shook hands with Osmo, Zethra and Badru before they joined the king.

The five hundred prisoners were making their plea for their lives. Lundar, Theodess and Aziel were trying to decide the fate of the prisoners.

Upon his arrival, King Darr was asked what to do with the five hundred. He ordered silence from all those close enough to hear his voice.

King Darr walked into the middle of the encircled prisoners and stood alone and silent for a moment before he spoke.

"Long before the grandfathers of any one of you walked in this land, I was king of Danann. It was not always so as you all know. When my homeland of Torren in the third realm fell to Adierach, I crossed the ocean to keep the philosopher's stone safe.

"I crossed to live in peace in a peaceful place. All of you here today have known me since your birth. Yet many of you chose to be my enemy when I never chose to be yours.

"So be it… You have chosen the ill will of Adierach so to Adierach you shall go. Lundar, lead them to the eastern shore and give them one ship."

One of the prisoners quickly said to King Darr. "Thank you for letting us live."

King Darr replied to the man. "Live… I knew where I was going so long ago, and it took fifty years to get here. How long will you wander at sea because you do not know the way?"

Lundar nodded. He was pleased with the king's demand. All five hundred stuck with one another for so long would be a much harsher punishment than death.

Lundar explained to King Darr. "It will take some time to do this. I will try to catch up with you in Anglamora.

King Darr said to him, “No. I wish for you and Theodess to remain here in Danann. Oversee the rebuilding both structurally and spiritually.”

Theodess quickly responded. “King Darr, I have sworn and oath to Anglamora for what has been done for me. I was called an Anglamorian.”

“Then you must keep your oath to Anglamora my good friend Theodess. Aziel will stay and help Lundar. King of the eastern shore. That is unless Lundar feels the same way?”

Lundar responded. “I will always be grateful to the kindness of the Anglamorians. I will be an ally for all time, but I will not again, abandon the eastern shore.”

Theodess said to Lundar, “We cannot spare any men to help you. Yet you cannot lead hundreds of prisoners by yourself.”

King Lundar shook hands with Theodess before he said to him, “I will not be alone. There are thousands of widows and young fatherless boys who would happily help cast this evil from our homeland.”

King Darr said to them. “Then is settled. Theodess, rest your men. At first light of morning, we march toward Anglamora.”

Just as King Darr started towards the white castle, Aerenthia appeared beside him. Together they walked across the field.

“Anglamora has been informed that I will keep watch over your army as they march west if I have your permission to do so." Aerenthia said to him.

King Darr replied. "I would be honored to walk beneath your light... For now, please stay with these men. They admire you greatly. They need an inspiration among them."

Before Aerenthia could speak and before King Darr could take off again, a great sound could be heard in the sky. It was likened to the sound of a ship horn. Although, it was much louder and bolder.

"The horn of wrath." Aerenthia said in a low calm voice.

"Wrath... Indeed." King Darr said to her as he started again toward the castle.

Lundar, King of the eastern shore ordered the remnants of the red army on their feet. The prisoners were marched to the base of the northern mountain where they were forced to dig a mass grave for their fellow conspirators and traitors.

Theodess and Aziel began recruiting the widows and young men who would join them. All who were physically able gave allegiance to the cause.

Soldiers of the white army searched the city through until the sun began to set gathering or killing all who wore red. Even so much as a red wrist band would get a person arrested.

Aziel had ordered ten men to gather every chain they could find. After hours of searching, just enough chains were brought back to chain the prisoners together in groups of fifty.

Aerenthia made her way to the northern mountain just before dark to speak to King Lundar.

"I will keep watch over the prisoners. Tell the others to rest. Tell them to find comfort in my light and sleep."

King Lundar bowed his head and took off toward the men still working the battlefield.

Aerenthia began to glow as she said to the prisoners chained together.

"You will not be able to escape my watch or my wrath. To try is a fool's hope."

She turned into the star and floated high in the sky over Danann. The prisoners kept digging.

Soon, small fires burned and the men who fought in Danann slept on the ground. King Darr looked on from the window of his chamber.

Fifteen hundred of his men lie sleeping in the dirt and bloodied grass with little to eat. The widows of Danann quietly searched the field for their loved ones to take them for burial. The rest were hauling the fallen soldiers of the red army on carts to the northern mountain.

King Darr could only shake his head at the scene. He looked to the star casting light over them before he quickly turned around.

A teenage boy was at the door of his chambers with tears on his cheeks. King Darr walked to the middle of the room before he told the boy to speak.

“My father perished in the battle. I was asked to help King Lundar.”

The boy paused, hesitant to say what was on his mind. It did not go unnoticed.

“What of your mother child?” Asked King Darr.

The boy replied. “She died during my birth. I have no one in this world now.”

“You are a child of Danann. This makes you a child of mine. I will ready you a room here in the castle.”

The boy appreciated the offer with a nod but King Darr could see something else was on his mind.

“Say what is on your mind child. Do not be afraid.” King Darr demanded.

The boy quickly replied. “I want to fight. I want to join you in the war to the west.”

The heartbroken boy had a pleading look as he waited his king’s answer. King Darr did not make him wait.

“You can help defeat this evil by helping to cast it out here.” Said King Darr.

The boy asked. “If Luciftias wins, will he spare me due to my age?"

"No." King Darr said with squinted questioning eyes.

“Then why must I be spared from fighting his armies?” The boy asked.

King Darr asked the boy for his name. He told the king his name was Nathaniel Redstone, son of Nathan Redstone of the southern mountain miners.

King Darr said, "So be it, Nathaniel. Because you would not be spared by the darkness, I ask that you spare not one of them. If you can follow this order, you may fight by my side."

The boy was overwhelmed by the king's understanding. King Darr led him to a fur covered bench next to the wall.

"Sleep child. Tomorrow we march to war." King Darr said with a determined voice and look.

CHAPTER 7

High on the western mountain of Danann, Osmo, Zethra and Badru walked alone toward Anglamora.

Osmo said to the others, "I thought Lady Starlight would guide us tonight."

Zethra replied. "I'm sure she has a reason not to be here."

A familiar voice said to them, "I am here to see you safely home."

The trio turned around to see the Grim Reaper standing behind them.

Osmo said to him, "Always happy to see you John, but if I'm not mistaken, you are not allowed to kill in battle. You would not be able to help us if we were attacked."

John Porter replied. “You are mistaken. The deal was broken, so the deal was broken. We followed the deal made by Evelyn Murray. That made the men and powers beholden to Luciftias bound to the deal he made. When he broke the deal, the rules changed.”

Badru said to John, “In that case, we are happy to have the harvester of life on our side.”

Osmo said to John. “I believe I can speak for us all when I give my condolences such as it is for Katie Carpenter.”

Zethra and Badru both nodded and John thanked them.

Zethra asked. “What of your friend the Undertaker?”

John replied. “He is with Mountain Max and Mateo crossing into Anglamora now.”

The Gatekeeper and the reaper Mateo had reached the border of Anglamora on top of the mountain. There the Undertaker was waiting for them. He was still wearing his black armor and gripping tight to the large double bit axe.

The Undertaker asked. “Mind if I ride with you?”

Mateo being much smaller than Mark, jumped in the back of the wagon and sat on top of the doors and gates stacked there. Mountain Max scooted as far as he could to one side and invited Mark to join them.

The old buckboard was barely wide enough but it done the job of carrying both.

Max said to Mark. "I am deeply sorry to hear about Katie. I know you too were good friends."

Mark replied. "Thank you. It's the first time I have seen the Mediator take someone himself."

Mateo asked. "Is the Mediator going to bring back Evelyn since the deal was broken?"

"He will if Katie can find her across the plane." Explained Mark.

That night was a long night for many who were restless or walking toward the center hut in Anglamora. The night was not long enough to heal the fatigue of thousands who fought the day before.

Max, Mateo and the Undertaker arrived at the firepit outside of Evelyn's hut before anyone else.

Max said to his companions. "There is nothing we can do here for now... What we can do is go to the cave and bring back food."

They traveled east to the road that turned north toward the cave. That is where they ran into John Porter, Badru, Zethra and Osmo.

Max addressed them. "My good friends. We are going to the cave cellar to bring back food for the coming crowd. A fire should burn at the pit for our guests."

Osmo said in a low voice, "I have not eaten in two days... None of us have."

The Undertaker got off of the wagon and said, “Then you three ride with Max. There will be something you can eat on the ride back.”

“The Druids fed me well, someone should take my place.” Mateo said to them as he jumped off the wagon.

So it was that Osmo, Zethra and Badru accepted to go with Max. Mateo, John Porter and the Undertaker would walk back to the firepit and wait for others to arrive.

The rise of the morning sun was upon Danann. King Lundar and his newly acquired army of young men, women and widows were on their way to the eastern shore.

The Anglamorian and white armored army had formed a line of two thousand men and strong women willing to fight.

Twelve wagons with each being pulled by six horses were at the end of the line. Each of the wagons were loaded with food and barrels of clean water. There was no room for riders or weapons on them. King Darr knew the amount of food it would take to feed so many for just a short time.

At the front of the line leading the army over the western mountain was King Darr, Aerenthia, Nathaniel, Aziel and Theodess. Old Toby flew overhead keeping watch while carrying a boulder in each foot.

“At this pace, it will be night when we reach the center of Anglamora… Possibly into the morning hours.” Aerenthia said to King Darr.

He replied. "I will move them slow and let them regain their strength. You said we have two weeks until the armies of Adierach reach Locklure. We need only ten to get there."

Luke and the Grave Digger, Sanwren walked behind the last wagon to keep watch at the back. Luke was periodically sneaking a cup of wine from a barrel at the end of the wagon.

At one point he said to Sanwren, "It is my payment for killing so many red army soldiers."

Sanwren held out his arms to his side. Luke grinned and said, "Your payment?"

Luke climbed on the wagon and opened a barrel in front of the wine barrel. From it he took out a loaf of bread and threw it to Sanwren. Afterwards, Luke filled a cup full of wine and handed it to his friend.

"Here is your payment Sanwren. I would give you more, but a man your size would drink the barrel dry." Luke said jokingly.

Sanwren shoved him with one arm and both men laughed. They seemed odd to all the rest marching with King Darr. Their oddity was, it seemed they were happy to march to their doom. Happy, so long as the enemy had plenty of men to stand against them.

The day wore on, and the few who waited in Anglamora began to wonder about King Darr and his army. John Porter decided to go see and report back. Osmo and Mark seized the opportunity to tease John about just wanting to see his girlfriend.

Before disappearing, John said to Osmo. "What it is to be in such good grace you can tease the Harvester who is now unbound from the rules."

Osmo's eyes grew wide, John disappeared and the Undertaker laughed at Osmo.

"I never even thought about it." Osmo said to the rest.

Max shook his head at Osmo and poured him a drink from the wine barrel.

King Darr and company had reached the top of the mountain bordering Anglamora. Just as the front four topped the mountain, they seen John Porter standing at the dividing snowline.

Aerenthia ran to him and held onto him as if it were the last time she would see him. Once she realized what she was doing, she glanced at the men behind her and let go of John.

"I'm happy to see you too." John Porter told her.

Aerenthia was slightly embarrassed but done well to hide it.

King Darr, Theodess and Nathaniel stood close by and John continued.

"We were beginning to let our minds wonder, causing unnecessary worry. So, I had to come see if all was well."

"Your concern for us is not without appreciation. We have many miles to go. I do not want this army too tired to fight." King Darr said to him.

Theodess asked. “Any news about Evelyn’s return?”

John replied. “None yet. I do not suspect there to be any until we meet the Mediator in six days.”

“I hope to be in Locklure in six days.” Said King Darr.

John grinned and said, “I can see you there much faster if need be. A friend, a gatekeeper can open a gate for you that will save you many days of marching.”

John paused and looked around as the army began passing him by.

“Where is Luke and Sanwren? Where is King Lundar?” Asked John.

Theodess replied. “King Lundar has returned to the eastern shore where he will remain.”

Aerenthia followed up. “Luke and Sanwren elected to bring up the back behind the wagons. They said it was so they could guard the wagons, but we suspect it is so they can drink without notice.”

John grinned and said, “I am willing to bet that is right. Although, that is a small price to pay to have them fight.”

King Darr quickly replied. “Yes. I agree.”

After his comment, King Darr ordered the army to rest for an hour before they descended the mountain into Anglamora.

Aerenthia and John Porter walked hand and hand through the army of brave men and women giving thanks to them for standing against the great evils of the world.

The sight of them together inspired all who could see them. Aerenthia alone was a sight to behold in her armor while knowing the power of starlight she possessed. All of them feared the Grim and the scythe that could burn through stone.

To the witnesses watching them pass by, it seemed there would be no way they could lose a war with such powers on their side.

Eight wagons from the end of the line, Aerenthia and John could hear Luke laughing and the Grave Digger's shovel hitting a wagon.

Luke was telling stories to Sanwren and both seemed to having a good time. The female driver of the wagon had a big smile on her face as she shook her head at John and Aerenthia. Whatever Luke was talking about it must have been funny.

When Aerenthia and John reached the two men, John asked. "Are you two drunk?"

Luke replied. "No. Drunkenness is unbecoming. You know that."

Aerenthia said. "It sounded like you were. Most are quiet and somber, yet you two are laughing?"

Luke replied. "I see. Maybe you have forgotten who we are. The Grave Digger has no candle and I was born with no fear. Unlike the other men here, I do not fear what has not happened and may not happen at all."

The female driver of the wagon grew a serious look and turned her head to look at Luke for a moment. His words opened her mind to a new way of thinking. She found comfort in his philosophy.

Both John and Aerenthia gave thanks to the two men for their service.

Luke said to them. "We are beyond that in our friendship. All I ask is from you, Lady Starlight. One day, you will have to lay down your swords so you and I can fight. Not in anger, but just for the sake of it."

Sanwren nodded, John smiled and Aerenthia replied. "As you wish, but I don't want to hear any crying when it happens."

Sanwren couldn't speak but he could laugh and he did as he pushed and pointed at Luke.

"You are more man than I for wanting to try Luke." John said with a smile.

Aerenthia grinned and winked at Luke who said to John. "She's a good one. You better keep her. At least another week or two anyway."

John looked at Aerenthia before he said, "I intend to."

John and Aerenthia returned to the front of the line just as King Darr was preparing them to march.

Aerenthia stayed to provide additional safety to the army and the Grim returned to the firepit where a new person was waiting.

The Druid King, Eshnar was standing in his white robe talking with the Undertaker when John appeared before them.

The small crowd looked to John Porter who told them the army of Danann was crossing into Anglamora and would be at the firepit late in the night.

“Then I will stay another day. I want to meet King Darr for the first time in more than a thousand years.” Said Eshnar.

John looked toward the hut and saw Osmo sitting in the chair by the door. He was leaned back and lightly snoring. John grinned at the sight of him.

“He got his belly full.” Zethra said to John with a smile.

John lowered his eyes for a moment before he said, “I remember how good it was to sleep. Even though I do not get sleepy as the Grim, I miss it.”

Eshnar addressed John. “I have assembled all that I can in Locklure for the coming war at the ice wall. We are over seven thousand strong.”

John glanced at the others who had the same concerned look as he did.

“I thought you would have more men available King Eshnar?” John asked.

Eshnar replied. "As I understand it, my seven thousand is far greater than the two thousand who march with King Darr."

"Twelve thousand stood loyal to King Darr on this hour one day ago." John said to Eshnar.

The Undertaker said to them both, "This is not a game of numbers. The numbers do not matter. The quality of the soldier and their level of training is what matters. We will win."

Eshnar asked. "How can you be so sure my good friend?"

Mark looked directly at King Eshnar as he replied. "Luciftias will not stand out front and lead his army. He will lead from behind as cowards do. That means, King Eshnar of Locklure, I will have to kill them all to get to him."

Zethra put her hand on the Undertaker's shoulder and looked him in the eyes.

"I will do my best until I draw my last breath to clear a path for you." Zethra said with a sincere voice.

Badru followed. "I will join her to make the path wide."

Mateo added. "You can count on all of the reapers to get you to him."

The red glow of the scythe did not unnoticed. Mark looked to the John Porter, Grim Reaper who said, "And I am unbound."

King Eshnar did not feel the same the way. He said to them, "I once heard it said, vengeance is not ours."

Zethra replied. "Not against our fellow man... Luciftias is not our fellow man."

CHAPTER 8

As the conversation continued among friends at the firepit, King Darr and his men marched on. The druids of Locklure began their march toward the great prairie north of the lonely black mountain.

Destiny, Fate and Karma kept watch as the events unfolded around them at the black mountain. The Timekeeper kept glancing at his clocks while sitting next to his fire.

Shadow reunited with Luciftias, returning him to his full strength as his armies marched across the ice.

King Lundar reached the eastern shore where a ship was making sail as the inhabitants of the eastern shore called Shorelingers watched.

As the ship began to fade from sight, the Shorelingers all looked to King Lundar in silence. He lowered his eyes and said in a low voice, "Okay... Home will still be here."

The mediator kept Katie in his arms as he sat in a chair next to the sarcophagus of Evelyn Murray. Katie's right hand, closed to a fist rested in his. Erissa kept the foamy pink blood wiped from her lips.

Katie Carpenter, mother of Tom Carpenter and mystic had begun her journey across the plane of time.

She started with the Timekeeper as her voice could be heard calling to him from his coffee pot. The old man took the pot from the fire and removed the lid. When he looked in, it was not his reflection looking back. He found himself looking at Katie.

"I need one of your watches. I need one missing three seconds." Katie told the old man.

The Timekeeper took a small pocket watch missing its chain from his own pocket.

"This watch was a gift to me from Evelyn Murray. It is very old and is the first to miss the three seconds. Have her give it back to me." The Timekeeper demanded as he dropped the watch into the iron pot.

The Timekeeper put the lid on the pot and sat it back on the fire. He leaned back for a moment before he said to himself. “What a task it is to find Evelyn Murray through all her long years.”

Lady Fate appeared across from the Timekeeper.

“It is a mountain Katie must climb if she is to save the world.” Fate said in a somber tone.

He asked. “What do I owe to be so honored by the presence of Lady Fate?”

Fate replied. “You are too kind. There is no debt. The watch you gave to Katie… I remember when I gave it to Evelyn. Before you ask, I will tell you, even I do not know how the seconds are missing.”

The Timekeeper said to her. “I once heard it said that all things have a fate. I do not ask my own. I ask if you have given a fate to Evelyn Murray?”

Lady Fate replied. “I did and she fulfilled it. If she returns, I will have a new one for her.”

“Which is?” Asked the Timekeeper.

Lady Fate answered. “My sister says she is destined to be the eighth inspiration. I say she will never again return to Moderna. It will be John Porter who propels her to the eighth status. My mother says Evelyn Murray is the karma of all dark things. The Mediator says, it is the darkness who gave us Evelyn Murray as all things must have an equal. Therefore, Evelyn created Luciftias. Her fate you ask… In this realm, Evelyn will have to come to terms with what she is to defeat Luciftias."

The Timekeeper's eyes were wide as he could not believe what he was hearing.

"My God… You three should really leave things alone." He said to her.

Fate smiled and said, "We are only a time from choices made. Nothing more. Speaking of time, I need a watch. I prefer the one you gave to Katie Carpenter when it is returned to you."

The Timekeeper nodded and Fate disappeared. He poured himself a cup of coffee and leaned back in his chair. Again, he couldn't stop from glancing at the clocks as if he were waiting on something.

Katie dialed the old watch back to the beginning. She found herself in Adierach and could see the Mediator walking with young Mark. Evelyn was nowhere to be seen.

Katie tried speaking to the Mediator, asking if he knew where Evelyn was. Neither the Mediator or Mark could see or hear her.

The hot winds blew hard in that forsaken land. Katie tried dialing the watch back further, but it would not turn anymore.

"She must be forward or a place backwards I cannot get to." Katie said to herself.

She slowly dialed the watch forward and found herself on top of the ice wall. Again, she saw Mark walking alone with the Mediator.

Just as Katie began turning the watch dial, she could hear the faint growling voice of Luciftias say, “You will not find her.”

Frustration grew in Katie’s eyes, but she knew she must go on.

While Katie Carpenter searched for Evelyn Murray, King Darr and company finally reached the firepit in Anglamora.

King Eshnar and King Darr wasted no time in greeting each other. It was obvious they were two old friends seeing each other for the first time in years.

After the greetings were made by the kings and soldiers, a council gathered around the firepit as others ate and rested.

John Porter, the Undertaker and Aerenthia stood together. The seven reapers stood just past them to the left. On the other side of the fire, Theodess, Aziel, Nathaniel, King Darr and King Eshnar stood together. Mountain Max stood at the end where the two sides met.

King Darr addressed the group. “I was told there is a Gatekeeper here who can save us many days march to the northern prairie. I would like to meet this man.”

All of the rest pointed at Max. King Darr bowed his head to Max before addressing him directly.

“I do not doubt the man who told me you can do this. If you so choose to help us, we will be in your debt.”

Max replied. “There will be no debt. I have had a gate to Locklure for a long time. It doesn’t take much to set it up and open it.”

Eshnar said to them. “If it is needed, there is a road to the top of the black mountain. We can retreat there and have the high ground.”

Mark quickly said to Eshnar. “There will be no retreat.”

Theodess nodded at Mark and simply replied with an “aye,” to show his agreement.

Aerenthia said to the group. “I will go see how far the enemy is from the prairie.”

John quickly said, “No Aerenthia. It does not matter at this point. We know they are coming.”

“We should crowd the ice wall. They will be slow coming down and their numbers will count for nothing.” Said Badru

King Eshnar replied to Badru. “You ever heard the term, shooting fish in a barrel? Arrows would rain down upon us until we were all dead.”

Young Nathaniel mustered the courage to speak among his leaders.

“If it were me, I would spread our line thin, let them break through and then circle them.”

King Darr glanced at the boy and replied. “It would work if we had the numbers. Our combined nine thousand is not enough to circle their fifty thousand.”

The Undertaker said to them, “We are five days out from going to the eternal cemetery together. That means those of us with special powers may not be there for the first charge of the fight. We don't know what the Mediator wants from us."

Aerenthia said to Mark. "Then let's go fight him right now. John and I could have killed that creature once before. We can do it again."

King Eshnar said to her. "You are an inspiration to all these men. Should one thing go wrong, and you not return..."

King Darr agreed with Eshnar. "We do not doubt your capabilities Lady Starlight. We just cannot afford to lose you."

Aerenthia replied. "With war comes loss and sacrifice."

The Undertaker responded to her statement. "Evelyn Murray made the sacrifice. Katie Carpenter and thousands of Anglamorians were lost. We understand. We must all fight this war together."

John Porter said in a low voice. "Together."

King Eshnar lightened the mood by saying, "Let us feast and enjoy the night with our companions and warriors. There will be time for these discussions."

The others agreed. Their conversation ended just as the last wagon came through. Luke and Sanwren had emptied a barrel and were riding on the back of the wagon.

King Darr saw them and shook his finger as he said, "Lazy!"

Mark and Theodess laughed. John was still in deep thought and Aerenthia knew it.

"She will find her John Porter." Aerenthia said to him.

John replied. "I do hope so... I just wonder, outside of this realm, what would it matter? Who would ever know the deeds done here?"

Destiny appeared beside John and Aerenthia.

She said to them, "Walk with me."

Destiny lead them down the cobblestone road along the white trees toward the prairie west of the hut.

Destiny said to John. "You are from Moderna and to Moderna you will return when this war is over. You will tell our story to the world."

Aerenthia said to Destiny. "If he is to return to Moderna, I will relinquish my starlight and join him."

Destiny asked. "Even if it would mean to never again see Anglamora?"

Aerenthia replied. "Yes."

Destiny looked around as they walked before she continued.

"This forest is so pretty at night. The white trees and the lake will forever be a reminder of the star who once saved us all."

When they reached the edge of the prairie, Destiny continued once more.

"Luciftias is much closer than you think. He will be at the edge of the ice wall in three days.

You must convince the reapers and powers to be in the Eternal Cemetery tomorrow."

John asked. "Are you sure Katie will find Evelyn Murray?"

Destiny grinned as she looked across the prairie. John and Aerenthia anxiously awaited her reply.

"Katie and Evelyn are across the plane of time. Time my good friends is all I am, based on decisions people have made. I too can travel there." Destiny told them just before she disappeared.

John took Aerenthia's hands in his, the scythe stood on its own.

"I cannot ask you to forfeit the starlight. Though I dream of living a normal life with you, I will not ask you to sacrifice so much."

"Then don't ask me John Porter. I would not ask you to do the same. I choose to on my own accord. Same as you would do. When this war is over, take me to Moderna. I have longed to see it for myself." Aerenthia said to him.

John replied. "Katie's home and farm will pass to me. I will take you there when this war is over. Never again will you wander because I will take you home."

Zethra and Osmo were also on the road heading to their home for the night. John and Aerenthia seen them and nodded but no words were spoken.

Lady Starlight and the Grim Reaper returned to the firepit area where John joined Mark, King Darr and King Eshnar who were speaking to each other.

"I have been informed that Luciftias is only three days from Locklure. I was told, those who were requested by the Mediator be in the Eternal Cemetery tomorrow."

The other men were shocked and Eshnar asked. "Who told you this?"

John replied. "Destiny."

Mark said to them, "So be it. Tomorrow we go."

"Aerenthia is informing the reapers." John told the other men.

The reapers joined the Grim and the two kings, Aerenthia went inside the hut. She was the first to do so since the Anglamorians returned.

The reaper Mateo said to them, "If we must go, let's go early and get it done."

Mark agreed and looked to Sanwren and Luke. They were leaned against each other with their backs against the wall of the hut.

Mark shook his head and the others laughed.

"I will wake Sanwren in the morning. He will have to bring that shovel." Said Mark.

John asked. "What of the white staff inside the hut?"

Mark replied. "We better bring it just in case."

As they spoke the door of the hut opened and Lady Starlight stepped out. She was not in her armor as many from Danann had only ever seen her. She was in her white gown and faintly glowing.

Her presence was impossible not to notice. Everyone in the open area grew quiet and watched her in awe. She had her hands together under her chin as she looked around at the crowd of men.

She said to them, “Rest now men of Danann, Locklure and Anglamora. I will keep you safe through the night.”

Her glow brightened slowly as she began to float upward. Once she was high in the night sky, she completely transformed into Anglamora’s most beloved star.

CHAPTER 9

While a deep sleep fell in Anglamora sparing only the Grim and Undertaker, Katie was hard at work across the plane of time.

Katie Carpenter had made it through Evelyn's timeline to the point she came to help Tom Carpenter.

She watched threw a window to see only a blur of the people she loved most. Katie could hear Tom and Kristi's voice but could not clearly see them.

Moments passed before Katie came to the realization, she could not see it because Evelyn was never there in physical form.

Katie could tell she was running out of time as well. "I have to think... Where would Evelyn go?" She said to herself.

Katie walked down the road from Tom's house for a while until she came to the old familiar light post. The light was still on and still shedding light on the old metal bench under it.

There Katie sat with down cast eyes. In her mind, she was failing. She let out a sigh and said to herself in a low voice, "Where is she?"

The voice of a friend came from beside Katie on the other side of the bench.

"The past cannot be undone. Evelyn Murray cannot seek refuge here."

Without looking up or to her side, Katie knew who it was.

"Destiny... I hoped you would come. If she is not in her past, then where is she?" Katie asked.

Destiny replied. "Beyond."

Katie asked. "Will you take me there? Will you take me to her?"

Destiny took Katie's hand and said, "Of course I will."

Katie freed her hand from Destiny and took out the watch to wind it. Destiny stopped her by putting her hand over the watch before she explained.

"That watch will not help you now. Only Evelyn Murray can move it forward that far. You will have to give it to her. When you do, and she returns, all the clocks missing the three seconds will have to catch up."

Once again Destiny took Katie's frail looking wrinkled hand in hers. Destiny gave Katie a wink and the two disappeared from the bench.

The two of them moved through time like being on the outer rim of a vortex. In this case it was a white vortex much like a massive white tornado. At the bottom was the fast pace of childhood and her time in Adierach.

As the vortex expanded upward, time moved slower, much like time on the ice walls. Each outer ring of ice, being larger has a slower time. One day in Adierach is One hundred years in Moderna.

Seeing the vortex from the eye on the inside, Katie began to think of Evelyn's claim of being oldest of them all. Katie's mind drifted to the first time she saw Evelyn Murray bring up a white tornado.

For Katie Carpenter it was all starting to make sense. She looked at Destiny as they floated upward and suggested.

"Her power is time. The lightning, storms, all of it is her time. She can separate herself from it, causing her time to be seen as a power. How is that possible Destiny?"

Destiny was looking beyond Katie as she said, "We're here."

Destiny seemingly reached out and grabbed one of the spinning rings of time and held on. Destiny and Katie found themselves standing in what used to be Katie's front yard.

It was raining heavily, and the place looked quite different. Although, what caught their eyes first was Lady Fate. She had beat them there.

Katie and Destiny slowly approached Lady Fate who was soaking wet, watching the door of the house.

When they got close to her, Fate said to the other two, "What took you so long?"

Destiny only grinned. Katie looked all around. The property was left to Katie by Evelyn once she was done helping Tom Carpenter. Evelyn had no intention of returning to Moderna for long periods of time.

Katie slightly shook her head as she said, "This place... I know this place, though it was never like this. Evelyn left it to me many years ago. I only left it days ago and now it looks to have been remodeled and changed.

Katie pointed to the new metal shop building beside the chicken coop as she said. "That building was not there."

Lady Fate said to Katie. "This place, here and now has not been yours for ten years."

Katie looked at Destiny who replied with only one word. "Beyond."

A moment later, a small blonde girl ran outside into the pouring rain carrying a basket. She was running toward the chicken coop. Lady Fate raised her right hand to the sky.

Destiny pointed her finger to a spot in the yard as she said in a low voice.

"As Fate would have it, lightning will strike there at this time. Now! Kill her!"

Katie yelled out, "No!". Fate brought her hand down and lightning followed hitting the girl.

Destiny immediately turned and wrapped her arms around Katie as she said, "You have to trust me now, Katie Carpenter."

Katie looked down at Destiny just in time to see a pecan shell hit the ground. The Mediator had come to join them.

Destiny kept one of Katie's hands in hers as she led the old frail woman to the little girl who was laying on the ground.

Destiny said to Katie. "Only death can stop time in the form we have. Give the watch to my sister."

Katie done what she was asked and handed the watch to Fate.

Destiny held her hand out and said to Katie, "Go to her."

Again, Katie Carpenter done what she was told. She walked to the girl and got down on her knees to lift the girl's head up against her chest.

Fate opened the watch to see the second hand barely moving as if it were moving in slow motion.

"We must hurry. One second has already passed."

The Mediator touched the little girl and she opened her eyes. The girl blinked multiple times before she asked. "Who are you?"

Katie said to her, “Friends child. We are your friends from another time.”

The girl asked. “What happened?”

Fate handed the watch to the little girl and said, “Take this watch. It will help you find us.”

The girl took the watch and began to look at it. Destiny said to her, “You have to come back now, Evelyn Murray.”

The girl asked. “Come back where?”

Katie took her last wooden nickel out of her pocket and held it in her hand for the girl to see. On the side that was up, it was engraved with the words, ‘one hug’.

Katie said to the girl. “A hug is priceless yet has no value in money. This wooden nickel is old and it has bought many hugs. It is to be given to someone you love and want to see again so the passing of the nickel continues.

“There is a place called Anglamora and the people who live there are very special. They need your help.

A man there who cares for you above all needs a hug from you. Pay him for it.”

The girl asked. “What is his name?”

Katie replied. “His name is John Porter.”

Tears instantly filled the girl’s eyes as she looked up at Katie.

Destiny fell to her knees and looked the girl in the eyes as she said, “Only death can stop time in the form we have. This place and time can wait. Return to Anglamora and your old form.”

The Mediator said to them, "Less than one second left."

The girl looked at him with a questioning look. He said to her, "If we do not return now, you die when the second hand moves again. I cannot force you to join us. You must choose to come back with me."

Destiny nodded at the girl and Katie said to her, "Do it for John Porter and yourself so you don't die."

The girl asked. "How? I will go but how?"

The Mediator said to her, "Turn the watch dial backwards."

Just as the girl began to turn the dial, the Mediator, Destiny, Fate and Katie held onto the little girl. When the dial turned, they disappeared from the spot in the yard where they were.

At that same time, inside the great tomb of the Eternal Cemetery, the sarcophagus of Evelyn Murray cracked like glass in many directions but did not fall apart.

Erissa let out a gasp and stepped back. The Mediator opened Katie's hand to find the wooden nickel missing. The Mediator smiled and touched the sarcophagus as he said, "Soon."

In the box canyon west of Locklure, the Timekeeper was awoken to a sudden silence. The clocks had stopped bouncing. They were stuck in place. He sat up and cleared his eyes to look at them again.

"She is in between." He said to himself as he got up out of bed. He poked the stick into the coals of the fire and said in a low voice. "You have to hurry Evelyn. You cannot stay there for long."

In Anglamora, John Porter and the Undertaker were sitting one on each side of the firepit. The fire had burned to ash with only a few coals glowing in the dark.

A strange breeze came up the cobblestone road that did not go unnoticed. Both turned to look down the road, but nothing was there.

Just as they turned back to face each other a small white swirl rose up from the firepit. Most who have sat around a fire have seen smoke, ash or fire swirl in a breeze. Never has it been white.

Both men wanted to believe it was a sign, but neither said anything. Afterall, they did not have to given the look in their eyes.

John asked. "You have been involved in death much longer than I. Have you ever seen anyone returned to life?

Mark replied. "No. My mother believed it was possible. The Mediator says it is... I hope it is."

John asked. "What do you think the Mediator wants with us?"

Mark thought about it before he replied. "If Shadow has returned to Luciftias, then the powers must be returned as well."

Aerenthia's voice came from behind them. "I was a star before there was an Anglamora, before any powers were given. What would he want with me?"

Mark replied. "I do not know Lady Starlight."

King Darr had awoken and overheard the words Aerenthia spoke. He crawled out from under the wing of Old Toby and joined them at the pit to offer an answer.

"Such a light... So bright even the dead can see it. You are a great power indeed. Word has crossed my ears of your battles here. I know you were for a time, restricted from returning to the sky. I was told you were the saving light in Evelyn's darkest hour. Some men say you are fury in physical form. I do not believe this."

You seek something that would be considered a destiny. A great destiny indeed. My new friend, Lady Starlight... Great destiny requires great sacrifice."

"The old one made the sacrifice for those she loved. So too John Porter and Mark have sacrificed. These men have paid a heavy toll and still pay.

"I believe you have it in your mind, starlight is your only power. I also believe this weakens who you truly are.

"Here at the end of this age, possibly the end of all things, you ask what Death would want from you... You, the only power in this realm not given as a weapon, but a light in everyone's darkness.

"The old one is lost across the plane of time and she will need a light in a dark place one last time."

Aerenthia did not like what she heard from King Darr though she knew he was right. Both John and the Undertaker knew King Darr spoke the truth as well. It was a hard truth for all of them to accept.

By this time, King Eshnar had awoken and come to join them. All nodded to him, and he returned the nod of respect to the small group.

"I must wake the men and prepare them. Daylight will be upon us soon." Said King Eshnar.

King Darr suggested. "Let them sleep until the powers have left this place. It will be easier for the men to wake to their absence rather than watch them leave."

Eshnar replied. "You are correct my old friend, but we must hurry."

Aerenthia went to the hut and retrieved the white staff. Mark, and the two kings woke the other powers.

Only a few minutes later, the seven reapers joined the Grim, the Undertaker, Sanwren and Lady Starlight.

They began to form a circle, their hands locked together. John Porter stood between the Undertaker and Lady Starlight. From her, the seven reapers were together with Sanwren at the end where he locked hands with the Undertaker.

Sanwren's shovel, John's scythe and the white staff leaned against their bodies. Mark said to the two kings, "We will not abandon you."

Before one of the kings could respond, the circle of powers disappeared.

King Darr said to King Eshnar. "Today we go. It seems all that we have done through all these long years was preparation for today."

King Eshnar replied. "I am honored to fight this evil at your side. How special it is to be here and now, with such a task bestowed upon us."

CHAPTER 10

The armies of Anglamora and Danann rose from their sleep to put on their armor and prepare to enter the prairie of Locklure.

With the help of Osmo and Theodess, Max got the gate stood and open. The soldiers of Danann had never seen such a thing as Max's gate. While it was open, they could see the grass and prairie on the other side of it. Each had to walk around the gate to look at it from the side. It only opened one way.

From the back or the sides, all that could be seen was the area they were in at the firepit. Then as they walked back around to the front, there was Locklure on the other side. Each soldier from Danann had to see for themselves.

Max thought it was rather funny. King Eshnar thought they were wasting too much time.

King Darr suggested letting the men enjoy the little things they could before such a great battle.

Four men at a time walked through and the wagons barely fit. It took nearly two hours to march the army through. King Eshnar led them into Locklure and King Darr with Old Toby was the last to step through.

King Darr asked Mountain Max. "Are you not going to join us?"

Max replied. "No. I was asked to make sure Anglamora is never uninhabited again. So here I will stay alone until you return."

As Max began shutting the gate, King Darr said in a rather sad tone. "Farewell Gatekeeper."

The gate shut and Max leaned against it with his fist clinched. After a moment, he calmed himself and said in a low voice. "So many brave men and women marching to their doom... I am left here in sanctuary to be only a witness, and only one can save them now."

The one Max spoke of was still resting inside the sarcophagus and in between with Katie Carpenter.

The little blonde girl and Katie were alone inside the vortex of time. Due to the disruption, there was no distinct ring to grab onto. Nor did the watch seem to help them while inside.

Each time the girl turned it, they moved up or down inside the vortex, but it was only a raging storm of lightning, thunder and mostly darkness.

Katie held tight to the girl who yelled out, "Where do we go!"

Katie replied as she held her tighter. "I do not know. We must wait for sign! We must wait for someone to show us the way!

The power of the Undertaker had transported the group to the outer steps of the great tomb. Mark opened the door and stepped inside. Erissa greeted them and introduced herself to the seven reapers before she led them down the hall.

Erissa was first to enter the chamber of the sarcophagus. Mark was second behind her. As he entered, he noticed the cracks covering the sarcophagus. He walked to the left of it and let his hand slide over the cracked stone.

The Mediator was sitting at the upper right side of the head of the sarcophagus. Katie was still in his arms.

The Mediator said to Mark, "It is wise you have come so early. She is fading fast into darkness."

John asked. "What do we do?"

The reapers, Sanwren and Aerenthia filled the room to circle the sarcophagus of Evelyn Murray. Each of them laid a hand on the cracked stone lid.

The Mediator said to them. "All of you have powers I have given except for one. The pendants were a gift. So too was the shovel, scythe, and the bell Anitoll.

"Evelyn is now dead in two places and alive within the storm of time. The clocks have stopped turning."

Aerenthia asked. "What does that mean? Tell us... What do we do?"

The Mediator continued. "Luciftias has reunited with all the powers bestowed upon the darkness. So too must the powers of light be returned."

The Mediator reached his hand through the side of the sarcophagus. The stone melted at his touch. From it he pulled out Evelyn's twisted staff.

He looked at Aerenthia and asked for the white staff. She handed it over and the Mediator melted it together with the twisted staff. It became one white twisted staff with the egg-shaped crystal on top.

Then the Mediator asked for the pendants. The seven reapers and John Porter handed over their pendants. The Mediator melted them in place in circles around the base of the crystal.

Next was the Gravedigger's shovel. It too was melted into the staff. It created a metal cap on the bottom of the white twisted staff.

The Mediator said to John Porter. "I need the scythe."

John handed it over without question. When the Mediator began melting it, the metal of the blade ran down the shaft of the white staff in two different spirals.

John asked. "Do all these powers remain within the staff?"

The Mediator replied. "Yes... They are all here within this one object. Now, I must ask each of you if you are willing to give these powers to bring back Evelyn Murray?"

Zethra answered immediately. "I am honored to give my pendant to see her return."

John followed. "I never liked that scythe. I am honored to see it returned."

Sanwren acted as if he were washing his hands and nodded at the Mediator. The other reapers expressed their willingness to give their pendants for Evelyn's return.

Mark said to the Mediator. "You have not asked for Anitoll yet... You need not to. I will forfeit the bell and my position to see my mother's return and defeat of that awful creature."

The Mediator said to Mark. "So be it. You will retain your power until you are in Locklure. Once you enter, you must ram the bell Anitoll. When you do, it will be undone.

"The power of the Undertaker will be returned to Destiny. So too will the power of the Grim and powers of the reapers."

The Mediator looked at Aerenthia but remained silent... After a moment, Aerenthia asked the others to leave her alone with him. Even Erissa was asked to leave.

Once the room was empty, Aerenthia said. "You want my starlight."

The Mediator replied. “I have no use for your light.”

He pointed at the sarcophagus and said, “But she does.”

Aerenthia shook her head and said, “She is a Mystic… She cannot wield the power of starlight.”

“Not her.” The Mediator said as he handed the white staff to Aerenthia.

She asked. “How will putting my starlight into this staff help bring back Evelyn Murray?”

“She is in a dark place right now Aerenthia. Where she is, I cannot go. Evelyn is between memory and dream in a time that may or may not even happen. Katie is keeping her alive and from disrupting the vortex of time. She has no reference to cling to.”

“I cannot ask for your starlight if you are not willing to give it. If you do, understand Aerenthia, it will not be like before. You will never again return to the sky. You will be a mortal woman only.”

Aerenthia replied. “Tell me what to do.”

The Mediator wasted no time. “Place your starlight into the crystal. Then take Katie’s hand in yours. She will show you the way.”

Aerenthia cupped her hands around the crystal and paused for a moment as her mind wandered through her memories.

“We must hurry Aerenthia.” The Mediator said to her.

She replied as her eyes began to glow white. "Cover your eyes."

From outside of the room the fellowship saw the white light burst from the seams of the door. Its magnitude was so strong it turned the old oak door solid white and put a white scar on the opposite wall.

From down the hall the fellowship could barely look in the direction of the chamber holding Aerenthia.

Zethra said in a loud voice. "My God! She's doing it! She's giving up her starlight!"

Inside the vortex, Aerenthia found herself standing next to Katie Carpenter and the young girl. Aerenthia was holding Katie's hand and would not let go.

Aerenthia said to them, "I was told you needed a light in a dark place."

The young girl asked. "Are you here to help us?"

Katie replied to the girl. "She is Lady Starlight. Anglamora's most beloved star."

The little girl reached her hand out and took Aerenthia's hand in hers. She looked at Lady Starlight with a slightly confused look before she calmed.

She said to Aerenthia. "From the air she came... Aerenthia. I remember you. Such a gift to us, I could never forget."

The girl's words filled Aerenthia's eyes with tears. Aerenthia smiled and nodded before she said to the girl. "I have always been a light for you Evelyn. Now I need you to be a light for me."

The vortex began to stabilize. The more it did, the more the little girl aged right before their eyes. A white ring formed in the outer band of the vortex and an old woman stood where a little girl once did.

Evelyn Murray had returned to her old form. At the sight of her, Aerenthia let her tears of happiness flow as she reached to hug Evelyn.

Evelyn pulled Aerenthia's head down onto her shoulder.

"I'll never be starlight again mother. I'll never return to the sky or be able to be a light for you again." Aerenthia said through her broken voice and tears.

Evelyn replied. "She is Aerenthia... From the air she came... And she will always be my most beloved star."

Evelyn slightly pushed Aerenthia back so she could see her before she addressed her.

"You must return now, Aerenthia. I have work to do before I can join you. I must take Katie home first."

Aerenthia hugged Katie Carpenter who said to her. "Goodbye Lady Starlight."

Katie pulled her hand free from Aerenthia's leaving Aerenthia standing in the chamber. Her light was swirling like a white tornado inside the crystal of the staff.

The Mediator was gone from the room. Katie's body was lifeless as it leaned against the wall. Small pieces of stone fell from the sarcophagus to the floor.

Aerenthia took a moment to look around. The room was pure white from the intensity of her light. Even Katie's clothes had turned white.

When Aerenthia stepped out, John was there waiting for her. She wrapped her arms around him.

He asked. "Are you okay?"

Aerenthia replied. "I will be. I got to see her... Evelyn Murray. She remembered me."

Zethra asked. "What did she say? Is she coming to join us? Will she return?"

Aerenthia answered. "She is taking Katie home before she returns. For now, we must go and join the fight."

The Undertaker said to them. "Our hearse is ready. Time is different here. We must hurry."

Erissa joined the fellowship as they exited the tomb and walked toward the hearse.

John asked. "Erissa are you sure you want to join us in Locklure?"

She replied. "I cannot stay here. Once Mark rings Anitoll, we will never again be able to come back to the Eternal Cemetery. So, if this be the end, we will go together. If we survive, we will be Anglamorians together."

The druid had the bell mounted once again on top of the hearse and the horses hitched for the last time. The fellowship of powers entered the hearse to join their companions in battle.

Evelyn Murray had taken Katie Carpenter to the lamp post and bench in Tom Carpenter's realm across the plane of time.

Under the light of the lamp, Evelyn said to Katie. "This is where I must leave you my dear friend."

Katie looked up at the lamp and nodded before she replied.

"Such a journey it has been. Now our adventure together ends where it all started so long ago."

"It is the coming full circle of life and death. The cycle, those three deities are so proud of." Evelyn said to her.

Katie gave Evelyn a hug for the last time. Evelyn pulled the wooden nickel out of her pocket.

"Let me pay you for that hug my friend." Evelyn offered.

Katie smiled and replied. "No. Tom owes me one. You keep that one. Give it to John Porter when the time is right."

Evelyn nodded before she asked. "Will you say hello to Tom and Kristi for me?"

Katie replied. "Yes of course."

Katie began to walk down the road but did not make it far before she turned around and said, "Goodbye Evelyn Murray."

Katie began walking again but was able to hear the words of her friend. "Goodbye my friend, Katie Carpenter."

CHAPTER 11

Evelyn Murray was beginning to be whole again. The same could not be said for those in the prairie of Locklure.

The battle was underway… Time in the Eternal Cemetery was quite different. Three days had passed since the fellowship of powers left Anglamora. To them it was only a few hours.

The fellowship found themselves in the middle of the prairie. The armies of Danann, Anglamora and Locklure were north of them close to the ice. From their position, the fellowship could see hoards of enemy soldiers coming down the ice wall. The enemy had carved a one hundred foot wide staircase down the wall.

The Undertaker quickly climbed on top of the hearse and took hold of the ram behind Anitoll.

Lady Fate and Destiny appeared among the small group. Destiny addressed the Undertaker.

"Let the world hear the wrath of Anitoll one last time!"

Upon her words, the Undertaker pulled the ram back far. He shoved it forward at a great speed with all his strength. Anitoll answered.

It was not like the sounds it had made before. Its knell was deep and thunderous. The impact cast out a terrible shock wave that left none standing in the prairie.

When the shockwave hit the ice wall, it collapsed more than three hundred feet deep and as far as the eye could see in both directions. Thousands of enemy soldiers were killed in the collapse.

The knell was loud throughout the world. Even in Moderna people thought a bomb had been dropped nearby.

Lady Fate said so the fellowship could hear her. "They were meant to be standing on and near the ice at that time."

Anitoll melted into its former self as a chunk of the stone table. When Mark stepped down, the hearse disappeared. The armies stood up and looked to the fellowship just in time to see John Porter hug Lady Fate.

From his position near the front, Theodess said, "She really is on our side."

The devastation from Anitoll left both armies disorganized and out of place. Theodess gave the call to fall back.

Immediately, the armies of the three realms followed his orders and fell back to the fellowship.

The armies of the three realms and the armies of Luciftias took some time away from battle to regroup and re-access the situation.

John Porter and his group met with the two kings at the band of wagons off to their right. Zethra and Osmo ran to each other on one side of a wagon not far from the kings.

King Eshnar quickly asked. “What took you so long?”

John Porter replied. “To us, we were only gone a few hours.”

King Darr asked. “What of the old one? Will she return?”

Mark answered. “She will. When her work is done. For now, we must fight without her.”

Theodess said to them. “In any note, we are happy to have every able-bodied man… and woman.”

Aerenthia replied. “I am only a mortal woman now. I will do what I can, though it may not be much.”

Theodess made his way into the group and stood at the back of the wagon. He took hold of a blanket and before he removed it, he made a bold statement.

“My eyes see what others cannot. While you see yourself as a mortal woman. I see a lady I know called Fury.”

Theodess pulled the blanket off the wagon revealing Aerenthia's armor and swords stacked in a pile.

Aerenthia wasted no time and showed no shame as she immediately began taking her dress off. The men quickly surrounded her in a circle with their backs to her. John stayed with her and helped her get the armor strapped in place.

"She's done." John Porter told the others so they could turn back around.

Kind Darr said to Aerenthia. "You must let go of Lady Starlight. She does not exist anymore... Aerenthia can wait until this war is over. My friend, today you must be what brave men fear."

Aerenthia slightly grinned and pulled her swords as she eyed the enemy army gathering together.

Theodess looked at Aerenthia nodded and only gave one word. "Aye."

Aziel had come to join the group and report to the kings. "We are out of arrows. I estimate we lost more than two thousand in that first wave of attacks."

Aziel looked at Mark and said, "If you hadn't sounded that bell, we might not be here now."

"Yes we would! I was just getting started when that damn bell interrupted me."

Everyone smiled, knowing the voice and demeanor of their preacher, Luke. He was covered in blood and cuts with a gash above his right ear still dripping.

One of the women from the wagons quickly jumped down and began tending his wounds. Sanwren nodded at Luke who said to him. "Yes, I saved you a few. Although, if you had not showed up when you did, I was going to kill them all myself."

The former reaper Mateo said to Luke, "We believe you."

Most of the others laughed. Only one stayed focused on the enemy. Her eyes locked to the north. As the men spoke, Aerenthia stepped out away from them. She walked out past the line, keeping her eyes on her enemies.

Luciftias could see the glimmering armor in the distance. He knew who it was. Luciftias took the opportunity to step out in front of his forming line of men so Aerenthia could see him.

She kept her reserve, knowing she could not defeat him alone as a mortal woman. She also knew that Luciftias was most likely unaware of her lost power.

At the back of the wagon, Mark said to the kings. "We do not have to defeat them all, we only need to kill Luciftias. Let's focus our strength in his direction. Seven reapers, one Grim, one Undertaker, one Gravedigger and one star made a great sacrifice. Us eleven will work our way to him if your men can make a way."

Both kings nodded and Theodess quickly said, "I'll spread the word down the line."

Osmo said to Zethra. "Stay behind me until it is time."

She wrapped her arms around him and said, "Together."

Osmo replied. "Together."

Their words made John look for Aerenthia. When he saw her, he also saw the army of Luciftias preparing to charge.

"They're going to charge!" John said as he started toward Aerenthia.

Osmo yelled out, "Form the ready line!"

What was left of the armies of Danann, Anglamora and Locklure formed the line. Old Toby flew high overhead. King Darr kept Nathaniel at his side. Erissa stayed at the wagons tending to the wounded. Ten gathered around Aerenthia and looked at their ultimate foe Luciftias across the prairie.

A moment later, the loud voice of Theodess called out. "Make ready!"

Before he could give the sound to charge, a horn blew from behind them.

King Darr smiled and said, "I know that horn."

King Lundar of the Eastern Shore had come with all he could muster together. Lundar rode on horseback out front of the five thousand Shorlingers he brought to join the war.

Luciftias held off his charge. Likewise, Theodess waited on giving the order. It only took a few minutes for King Lundar and company to make it to join the line.

"In case you didn't know, Shorlingers are great bowmen." Lundar said with a grin.

His army marched in three lines. Infantry marched in the front with two lines of bowmen behind them.

King Lundar took his place among the other kings. Eshnar pointed at the eleven out front before he explained.

"We must make a path for them. They are going to kill Luciftias."

Lundar said to a man on his left and right what Eshnar said and told them to spread the word down the line.

The three kings were positioned directly behind the fellowship of eleven. Everyone was ready and waiting for the order to charge.

Nathaniel walked away from King Darr's side and made his way to stand beside Aerenthia.

Nathaniel asked. "May I shake your hand Lady Starlight? I have never seen a star so close until you came. If we survive this war, I would like to say I shook hands with you."

Not one word was spoken, or one sound made along the line as all watched Nathaniel's innocence on display without shame.

Aerenthia planted the sword in her right hand in the ground and took the boy's hand in hers.

"I was Lady Starlight but no more child." She said to Nathaniel.

He held onto her hand and replied. "I am Nathaniel. To me, you are."

Aerenthia shook her head and said, "Not today Nathaniel. Today I am someone else."

Nathaniel asked. "May I ask, what do I call you today?"

Aerenthia freed her hand and took up her sword. She looked across the field for only a second before she turned to Nathaniel to say only one word. "Fury."

Upon her word, she broke into a run toward the enemy army. Theodess sounded the order to charge. Likewise, the enemy army charged as Luciftias stood still. King Lundar pointed his sword forward and three thousand arrows took flight.

Aerenthia didn't make her charge for glory or titles. Nor was it for vengeance or blood thirst of her enemies. She made her lonely charge for John Porter as her mind replayed the moment he killed the person he loved as a mother. She charged for Katie Carpenter who came to a land where the old never die only to be murdered. Among her own and the steps of ten thousand men, she could only hear the words of the little girl. "From the air she came." Aerenthia charged toward Luciftias for Evelyn Murray.

From the top of the lonely black mountain, the three deities stood together. They could see Aerenthia's armor glimmering even under the shadow of waves of arrows being cast into the sky.

They watched as she led the last charge against the great evil of their time. She was not to be outdone and no one tried. The fellowship and armies of three kings began to form a V behind her.

Karma let go of a tear from her right eye upon the sight of it.

"That is what it takes to defeat great evil." Fate said as she watched.

Karma added. "Yes... That is why she is Shadow's karma."

Destiny said, "That is why she will always be remembered as Anglamora's most beloved star."

Karma, Destiny and Fate watched as the armies clashed together. The glimmer of Aerenthia's armor cut deep into the enemy lines.

Upon a sudden, Destiny cocked her head to the side as if something caught her attention. A brief moment passed, and she grinned just before she disappeared.

Fate said to Karma, "My sister is always up to something and never says anything."

Karma replied. "She didn't have to... Soon the world will know."

Theodess brought men up from the right side of the small group of eleven. Osmo took the left side where he could keep an eye on Zethra.

Aziel and Luke ended up together just outside of Theodess and his closest men. King Darr and King Eshnar moved in beside Osmo. They were staying tight together and trying their best to get in front of Aerenthia and the eleven. There were too many enemy soldiers to advance that far which left Aerenthia alone at the front.

King Darr shouted to King Eshnar. "I will go to her!"

King Eshnar nodded but was too busy fighting to talk. John Porter had only two short handled axes and was doing his best to protect Aerenthia's back. The other former reapers protected him.

Mark and Sanwren didn't bring a weapon. They used enemy soldiers instead. As axes swung at them, they would grab soldiers by the neck, pick them up and throw them into the others with incredible force.

In such tight conditions, it worked well to keep the enemy from being able to use shields to push. The bodies lying on the ground made walking difficult. Pushing while standing on them was near impossible.

Old Toby dropped huge boulders he grabbed from the black mountain on the soldiers nearest to King Darr. Luciftias took notice of the large worhawk and demanded an arrow.

A bowman near him shot an arrow toward the hawk and Luciftias guided the arrow with his staff. The voice of King Darr yelling "No!" rang loud as he watched his best friend tumble down from the sky. His priorities changed from joining Aerenthia at the front to making his way to Old Toby.

King Darr advanced toward the hawk with lightning speed. His movements and performance with his spear and dagger much resembled the skill of Aerenthia. King Eshnar stayed the course beside the eleven.

Osmo said to his men. “Go to King Darr! You must protect him!”

King Darr left a trail of bodies that was easy to follow even amongst the madness. Yet, there were still plenty more for Osmo’s men to fight.

As John and Aerenthia slowly moved forward with the other nine still behind them, the enemy soldiers began to stack up against them. Aerenthia was working her swords as fast as she could, but as a mortal woman she was running out of breath.

She slowed her movements only a small amount and it was enough. A soldier slipped by her and thrust his sword forward at John Porter. John moved and the blade went into Kenji’s neck.

The former reaper Josiah was close by and killed the soldier. There was no time for them to mourn for their friend or collect his body. They had to keep moving forward.

Luciftias was pleased with the death of Kenji and the death of so many from the realms he did not control. Once more Luciftias ordered his bowman to release an arrow. Again, when the arrow was released, Luciftias guided it with his staff.

The arrow was meant for Mark. The reaper Akeno reached far with his sword and barely clipped the arrow enough it missed Mark but entered Diego. Mark did not see Diego fall. He had a look of appreciation when he looked at Akeno who had a much different look. Mark could see the sadness in his eyes.

Mark turned around to see Diego lying dead at the back of the fellowship. He turned back around to face Akeno just in time to see another arrow hit Akeno in the back.

Mark grabbed him and eased him to the ground.

Akeno said to Mark before he died, “Kill him and be done with it.”

Akeno perished and Mark started to stand when the blade of an enemy soldier hit him in the shoulder. It cut his black armor but not him. The attempt on his life only made him mad. He grabbed hold of the soldier and folded him backwards until his head was between his feet. Then he picked the soldier up over his head and threw him into the others nearby.

Mark took the sword that cut his armor, Sanwren pulled an axe from another before killing him with it. Sanwren nodded at Mark as he motioned his head to move forward. The two giant men each grabbed a soldier, killed him, and then used the dead body in one hand as a shield while striking with the other.

They broke rank from the eleven and began moving up the side making their way toward Aerenthia and John. Theodess made room for them to quickly advance to the front. Luke had broke from his position in the back and was right behind Sanwren.

Aziel began to advance up the left side of the group with his best swordsmen with him. The enemy soldiers began to fall like dominos. Mark, Sanwren, Luke and Aziel had made it to the front next to Aerenthia and John who were gasping for air.

Badru grabbed John Porter and pulled him back. Luke began yelling Aerenthia's name as he got close to her so she wouldn't kill him. He had to grab her and carry her back into the center with John. At this point, John and Aerenthia were surrounded by friendly soldiers.

"You have done enough for now. Catch your breath." Luke demanded.

Both John and Aerenthia were unable to speak as they tried to stabilize their breathing.

Zethra stayed with John and Aerenthia, and all three of them could only watch as a small band of arrows came falling toward the fellowship. Zethra called out, "Arrows!" but the battle noise was too loud.

Badru and Mateo fell along with several of the soldiers near them. Aziel began waving his sword in the air. King Lundar took notice and ordered his personal bowmen to take out their counterparts.

The Shorlinger bowmen done their job well. Once Luciftias' bowmen were killed, he was left standing alone. Lundar ordered for the arrows to continue to fly. Luciftias began to back up as he blocked the barrage of arrows coming at him.

Mark and Sanwren kept up their attacks. They were in sync with one another as they thrust or swung the axe and sword, kicked the enemy soldier into the rest and step forward. Luke, Aziel, Theodess, Eshnar and Osmo cleaned up all who tried to attack from the sides. When the last two men fell in front of Sanwren and Mark, they were looking directly at Luciftias.

CHAPTER 12

Lundar noticed the two giant men had broken through the enemy lines. He ordered his bowmen to shoot faster and concentrate all their arrows on Luciftias.

Mark and Sanwren took off running toward him. Lundar stopped the bowmen. Sanwren threw his axe hard toward Luciftias knocking the staff from his hand. Mark dropped his sword.

To escape the arrows, Luciftias had to step forward and was met by two giant hands around his neck. Mark and Sanwren had hold of him. They lifted Luciftias high and slammed him to the ground with enough force he bounced more than a foot from the ground.

It was not enough... Luciftias quickly made it to his staff and stood up before the two men could grab him again.

Luciftias cast out a red shield and called out, with a loud growling voice. “Enough!”

His voice was heard by everyone, and the battle stalled. John Porter, Aerenthia, Zethra, Luke and Theodess stood beside Mark and Sanwren.

Aziel, Osmo and King Eshnar spread their arms out to keep the army back. King Darr walked out front of the armies to the side some fifty feet away as he watched with Nathaniel at his side.

It was noticeable to everyone including Luciftias that his army still greatly outnumbered the armies of the three realms.

Luciftias let his shield fade before he addressed them.

“You cannot win. How dare you challenge me.”

He began pointing his boney finger at them as he continued.

“An Undertaker with no bell. A Gravedigger with no shovel. A Grim with no scythe. A star that no longer shines and is weak. A reaper, the last reaper who has no pendant of light. A preacher with only the power to bleed.”

They all looked at Luke who was once again dripping blood from his wounds.

Luciftias continued. “And the last lonely nightwatchman. Who are you to challenge me?”

From the top of the lonely black mountain, Karma said to Fate. “Seven... Seven brave souls now stand against the darkness.”

Mark said to Luciftias. “The bell has tolled for you. You will die here in this field on this day.”

Aerenthia slowly began to position her swords. Zethra moved her daggers into position to advance.

Luciftias said to them. “You have stepped forward to challenge me. I accept. I will make a deal.”

Mark said before Luciftias could continue. “There will be no deals. No surrender.”

Luciftias replied. “As you wish.”

He lowered his staff in the direction of the seven. None moved a muscle. It confused King Darr who slightly shook his head. King Eshnar grinned at Darr.

Osmo let out a sigh of relief and whispered to himself. “It’s happening here before my eyes.”

Seconds passed and Luciftias grew restless. “What are you waiting for?” Luciftias growled at them?

Zethra relaxed from her stance and let her daggers fall to her side. Aerenthia also relaxed and let her sword tips touch the ground.

Luciftias was confused and angry. Once more he demanded as he asked. “What are you waiting for!?”

John Porter replied in a calm voice. “We are waiting for the eighth to join us.”

It was the words of John Porter that brought Evelyn Murray out of the vortex of time. At the same time John spoke those words, Destiny appeared at the great horn at the edge of Locklure.

Destiny put her hand on the shoulder of the druid who was stationed there. When he turned around, she said to him as she nodded. "Is my turn."

No one questioned Destiny in Anglamora or Locklure. The druid stepped away from the horn. Destiny stepped up to the mouthpiece which was at the bottom. The horn swirled and expanded as it went upward some fifty feet to the top. It was held in place within the tower of inspirations designed and built by Eshnar and the druids.

The top of the horn lay flat open to the sky and covered the entirety of the platform floor of thirteen feet in each direction.

Destiny took a deep breath and blew hard into the silver horn designed for Evelyn's return.

Not even Anitoll could match the magnitude of the sound it made. The druid standing as a witness, looked to the sky as if it were going to fall. The rocks of the mountain shattered and turned to gravel.

In the box canyon west of Locklure, the Timekeeper had his hands in a basket of whole kernel corn. The feed pale he put the corn in sat on a stump beside the basket.

When the horn sounded, the pale vibrated off the stump and stones on the cliffs fell. The clocks on the inside of the shed began to spin at a high rate of speed.

Faster and faster the clocks turned. "They're trying to catch up." He said to himself.

The Timekeeper walked out from under his covered shed, spread his arms out wide as he started laughing loudly.

"Welcome back Evelyn Murray!" He shouted toward the sky.

The speed of the spinning became too much for the clocks as they began to fly into pieces and burst apart.

The Timekeeper continued to laugh even as he turned around to see all the clocks busted with some gears still glowing red and burning holes in his bed. All the clocks busted except one.

The old watch he had given to Fate was swinging from its chain attached to a nail on the center beam of the shed.

The Timekeeper took down the watch and held it in his hand as if were the most fragile thing he had ever held. The second hand was moving forward like normal. Again, the Timekeeper began to laugh.

The force of the horn broke loose even more of the ice wall. An avalanche formed behind Luciftias forcing him to turn around and use his staff to hold back the snow and ice. At the first sight of the avalanche, the armies of both sides ran further south into the prairie to escape it. Seven did not run.

When the ice finally stopped, it formed a horseshoe around the small group and Luciftias. He stood with his back to them only for a second.

"Time is up." He said as he spun around and cast out a powerful red beam of hatred, malice and death at the group.

However, the power of his staff was stopped by a shield of powerful white light. Evelyn Murray was standing at the end of the line next to Luke.

She had returned to her old form wearing her old gray dress and dark grey cotton poncho on her back. Her hair hanged straight down at the sides protecting her face from the sight of the others.

She had the white staff standing as she held in in her right hand. Luciftias moved his staff over, so it pointed at her.

Luciftias said to her, "We finish it."

Evelyn slowly took the white staff in both hands and pointed it at Luciftias.

There was a brief pause and deafening silence on the field of thousands watching.

Evelyn replied. "We finish it."

The power of the staffs were no longer equal. In the instant the red glow form, Evelyn struck down the opposing staff with a beam of white starlight.

Upon seeing it, John took Aerenthia's hand in his. The red staff crumbled into pieces. Evelyn began moving toward Luciftias who was beginning to beg her to make a deal.

Evelyn said to him, “I made a deal.”

Luciftias called out for the Mediator and Evelyn Murray released all the powers she contained upon him.

First, she cast out the white starlight forcing Luciftias to cover himself under his cloak. There was nowhere for Shadow to escape. Next a dark cloud formed over them, and lightning came down in many steady streams to contain him.

Strands of Evelyn’s hair began to rise. A swirl of snow lifted from around Luciftias in a minor looking tornado. The lightning began to swirl around the outer rim and inside the eye of the tornado, burning Luciftias.

Evelyn’s eyes turned to starlight and blue streaks of lightning began to cover her body and come from the white staff. At this moment, she intensified everything.

The base of the tornado sped up and shrank to only the spot where Luciftias was. The streams of lightning tightened around the tornado focused on that one spot. Then halos of even stronger white light began descending the tornado causing explosions on top of Luciftias who was curled into the fetal position on the ground under his burning cloak.

The men of both armies dropped their weapons and watched in awe. Osmo took Zethra’s hand and held it tight.

Evelyn Murray intensified the powers faster and hotter as the halos of white light impacted harder against Luciftias until his cloak had burned away. Even the snow burned.

Luciftias had turned into a small childlike burning creature as he lay helpless without the protection of Shadow.

Evelyn continued to intensify the storm until a pecan shell hit the ground and the voice of the Mediator called out. “Evelyn stop!”

She did not respond to his command. Again, and louder the Mediator addressed her.

“You cannot kill him Evelyn!”

The storm instantly disappeared over Luciftias but not in Evelyn who looked at him and shouted back, “Why not!?”

The Mediator calmly walked to her and said, “Because he doesn’t exist.”

Evelyn and the seven behind her immediately looked to where the creature was laying before and he was gone. The storm of lightning and starlight faded from Evelyn as she stood silently looking where Luciftias was.

The Mediator continued. “All things have an equal my old friend... You created Luciftias long ago and it was you who gave him strength.”

The seven began looking at each other and very confused. Evelyn was also confused as she looked at the Mediator.

He continued. “Do you remember why you had to escape Adierach? I do. ‘I am Eve! Greatest of them all!' you use to say boasting about your capabilities. The king saw you as a threat. A person who could destroy his kingdom.

"Then you came here and what did you say? 'I am Evelyn Murray! Oldest of them all!' then you proceeded to put on a show of your powers once again."

"Your pride was all the darkness needed to create to you an equal."

John quickly said to the Mediator, "How dare you say such things to her!"

The Mediator replied to him. "Are you not also guilty? I am what monster have nightmares of... Do you not remember? I could say something regarding each of you."

The Mediator put his hand on Evelyn's shoulder and said, "It doesn't make you anything other than normal. All suffer from it at some point. You must teach them Evelyn... Teach them, humility is the eighth inspiration."

The Mediator began to walk away as Evelyn stayed silent with her eyes down as she pondered all that happened and was said.

Sanwren did not let the Mediator go two steps before he stuck his huge arm out to stop him. The Mediator looked at Sanwren who pointed to the leather mask on his face.

The Mediator nodded and said, "Take off the mask. I will keep my word to you."

Sanwren took off the red leather mask and stretched his mouth and wiggled his restored tongue.

The Mediator said. “After all these years, surely you have something to say.”

The big man took one step to his right and put his big right arm around Evelyn and pulled her in close to him before he said in a deep voice few had ever heard. “She has no equal.”

His words brought tears to Evelyn’s eyes. The other six standing by gathered around Sanwren and Evelyn with their hands on her.

The Mediator grinned as he replied. “I think you’re right.”

The Mediator vanished and Evelyn Murray had to be humble to face the others. There was no judgement in their eyes as they recognized their own foolish pride.

Mark rushed to give her a hug and welcomed her back. Then one by one the seven welcomed her back and give a hug of their own.

John Porter was the last. Sanwren stepped away to give John a moment alone with her. Evelyn gave John a quick smile but could see the pain in his heart through his watery eyes.

John hugged Evelyn and whispered in her ear what he could not say when he last saw her alive. “I love you mother.”

“And I love you John Porter.” She said to him.

John leaned back so he could see her. Evelyn kept her free hand on his arm. She looked across the prairie at the thousands both alive and dead. The men and women of Anglamora, Locklure and Danann cheered. The enemy soldiers left on the field remained silent and watched.

King Darr approached and addressed Evelyn Murray as he bowed his head.

"I am King Darr of Danann. The great men and women of Anglamora come to my aid. I joined them to repay that debt here today yet found myself in greater debt to you. I offer my services such as they are."

Evelyn hugged the boy looking King and replied. "The time of debts has passed. I ask only for your friendship King Darr, keeper of the philosopher's stone."

He replied. "Granted of course Evelyn Murray, mystic of Anglamora."

Aerenthia said to the group. "I am surprised Destiny isn't here. This is the kind of moment when she likes to appear."

Evelyn said to Aerenthia. "I think the time of Destiny, Lady Fate and Karma has passed. All things fulfilled. Now let us all return to our homes in peace. I need to see Anglamora and, I need a cup of tea."

Evelyn's mention of tea brought a calmness and comfort they so longed for in her absence. Counting King Darr, nine of them began to walk toward the huge crowd of men in the middle of the prairie.

Aziel said in a low voice but loud enough for the few men of Danann next to him to hear. "We will always remember the day King Darr walked alone with the eight inspirations of our time."

Osmo was close enough to hear and replied to Aziel. "Our grandchildren's grandchildren will know we too were here. We were their friends."

The captain of the enemy soldiers overheard the words of Aziel and Osmo. He went to Osmo and asked. "Would you take me to see her? I have laid down my weapons and ordered the same from my men. I would expect no less than for you to stand between us, but I would like to speak to her."

Osmo hesitated and looked at Aziel who also heard the request. Aziel said to Osmo, "I'll go with you."

The three men walked across the field alone to meet the nine.

Before Osmo could say a word, Evelyn opened her arms. He gave her a hug and King Darr introduced Aziel to her.

Evelyn looked at the enemy soldier who was wearing not much more than rags beneath his breastplate. His beard and hair were roughly cut most likely from a knife due to the long journey across the ice.

The soldier bowed his head before he addressed Evelyn.

"I am Palko, Chief Captain of the armies of Adierach. After what I have witnessed here, even though my men are still many, there can be no victory... Nor do I now feel there should there be for us.

"In Adierach many generations before I was born, the old kings spoke of you. They tracked you to the ice wall and eventually found the stairs.

"For generations, the people of Adierach were told about a great witch who killed our king and crossed the ice to build an army. An army designed to destroy us all.

"I can now see that is not true. We were ordered to follow Luciftias without question. I knew it was him who whispered darkness to our king, but he was still our king. What are we if we are not loyal to each other?"

Evelyn replied. "No one ever thinks they are the bad ones. I know, I did not so long ago. Go home Palko."

Palko said to her, "It is such a long journey across the ice. May we rest here for a while?"

Evelyn replied. "This is Locklure. Here King Eshnar makes the rules."

King Eshnar wasn't far away as he was coming to welcome Evelyn Back.

King Eshnar said to Palko, "You may stay here in the prairie as long as you are unarmed with the exception of twenty bows you will need to gather meat."

Palko bowed his head to King Eshnar before he gave thanks in his own way.

"We are still many and many among us are great craftsmen. We will be at your service upon your call."

Evelyn and her companions joined the rest in an area around the wagons. Evelyn was immediately surrounded by so many who were happy to see her once again.

It didn't take long for fires to begin burning with food being spread around. The wounded were fed first, then John Porter ate like he was starving since he hadn't eaten anything the whole time he was the Grim. Men of both armies soon began to speak to one another. Evelyn watched closely. It was the sign of peace she longed for.

Evelyn felt compelled to address the crowd compiled of four armies as she brought the staff close to her face.

"It is a lonely place to walk between the worlds with no one to talk to. I think about all the lives lost or brought to ruin on my quest through time. Unlike the deities who are a time, I am only a memory... A dream that has become a memory, an old story told.

"Now the quest is over yet the counted number of those lost still rise. Hold tight to their memory and they will never die. Hold tight to my memory so whenever the word mystic is spoken, you think of me. My journey here has been mystical indeed.

"Blessed are we whose tales are told. For us, the dream never dies. Let old grudges fade and love each other. In the end, when old structures crumble, we must take of care of one another.

"In the pages of our story, as long as the story is told, we remain… I will remain."

As Evelyn finished speaking her parable, she kept her eyes fixed on John Porter and Aerenthia. They felt as if she was speaking directly to them.

Everyone else stood silent trying to figure out what she was saying. Her words set a somber tone among the masses.

Evelyn walked to a nearby fire and sat down on an old wooden chair that had been strapped to a wagon for a long time.

Luke lightened the mood when he said to Evelyn, "I swear mother… First day back, you destroy the ice wall and confuse everyone. I think you need some juice from a barrel instead of tea. That tea isn't doing you any favors."

Only Luke dare say such a thing about Evelyn's tea or to her. His comment brought much needed laughter even to old Evelyn Murray.

Evelyn Replied. "Do you remember when you were little and I would threaten to turn you into a frog?"

Luke answered. "Yes. We all do."

Evelyn continued. "I can still do it Luke."

Their bond was unmistakable. It gave testament to Evelyn's willingness to both play and protect those she loved and viewed as her own. To be in her presence was to be comfortable as a child in their mother's arms.

CHAPTER 13

At daybreak the next morning, a wagon being pulled by a mule could be seen coming from the lonely black mountain.

Mountain Max had come to take Evelyn Murray home. All who were there watched Max cross the northern prairie of Locklure. It was the unspoken end to the conflict and sign that all must return home.

John and Aerenthia stood beside Evelyn as Max approached.

"I wonder who is in Anglamora?" Aerenthia said.

Max stopped beside them and smiled at Evelyn as he nodded.

"The Mediator returned the mystics to Anglamora from the great tomb where they were kept safe. They are waiting for you." Max said to Evelyn.

Something caught Max's attention and it didn't go unnoticed by the others. The turned around to see Old Toby stand up. The druid King, Eshnar was standing beside the worhawk petting his neck. King Darr had been asleep under Old Toby's wing.

King Darr stood up and asked Eshnar. "What magic is this?"

King Eshnar replied. "It is not magic. The arrow was restricting his blood. It was not enough to kill him right away but was enough to make him pass out. He was only sleeping with a low heart rate. I think he will be okay soon enough."

It was a miracle to all who watched the worhawk fall during the battle.

"Maybe King Eshnar can heal me too." Luke said as he looked over the bandages that covered most his body, face and head.

Sanwren said to him, "Most of us have wounds. You are a wound. Be careful next time."

Mark laughed and shook his head as he said to Luke. "Is that you in there Luke? All I can see is two beady eyes looking through bandages. Is there anywhere you aren't wounded?"

Luke replied. "Oh, you're real funny. My foot is not wounded, and I know just where to put it."

Luke's comment brought a much needed laugh to those standing by.

"Max, I think you may have come to give him a ride more so than me." Evelyn said continuing the jokes at Luke.

Luke replied. "Just prop me up by a barrel. I'll be okay."

"Yeah, you say that until you get drunk and fall out of the wagon. Then you will have more wounds to cry about." Mark said to Luke.

Sanwren quickly said, "Not if I am there with him. Someone must keep him from falling out."

Mark and Sanwren moved to each side of Luke who was sitting on a stack of firewood. The two giant men were careful when they helped Luke up and into a nearby wagon.

Luke quickly complained. "This is the wrong wagon. I don't see a barrel one in here."

People laughed as far as his voice carried. King Eshnar handed Luke a large corked jug made from clay and shells from the lake side. Luke pulled the cork, took a drink and instantly spat it out.

"What in the hell is that!?" Luke asked.

King Eshnar replied. "It's water. You don't need anything else while your wounds still bleed."

"Water... Might as well be poison." Luke said with great disgust.

Again, his comment brought smiles and laughter by those who could hear him.

While Luke was putting on a show for the crowd, John Porter and Aerenthia helped Evelyn onto Max's wagon.

Osmo had organized the men under his command to form a line to lead Max's wagon. Aziel formed a second line beside Theodess. Lundar and King Darr formed two lines behind the wagon.

King Eshnar stood with the druids, and they all bowed their heads in respect to Evelyn.

John, Aerenthia and Sanwren walked on one side of the wagon. Mark, Theodess and Zethra walked on the other side. Luke rode in the back. The eight stayed together.

While the Anglamorians and Tuatha De' Danann began their return, Fate was entering the box canyon to the west of Locklure.

Lady Fate appeared beside the covered shed. The fire in the pit inside of it had burned to ash. With no smoke bellowing out of it and with no closed sides, she could see everything under the roof.

On a small table beside the chair the Timekeeper normally sat in were small internal pieces of clocks. Only two of the many clocks inside were working. It was obvious the Timekeeper was putting them back together.

The watch she longed for was not anywhere to be seen. After a moment of looking around, she walked up toward the bluff.

There she found the old man on a wooden ladder cleaning the graffiti off the rock face. The words, "Three Seconds" were all over the rock face, and those words were being washed away.

The Timekeeper could feel her presence. He stopped wiping down the rock and looked at Lady Fate who was staring at him.

"They are not missing anymore." He said to her.

Fate replied. "No... Now we have the answer to the riddle. For Evelyn Murray, time doesn't count."

The Timekeeper nodded and climbed down the ladder. He took out the old watch and held it up.

"I suspect this is what you are looking for?" He asked.

Lady Fated replied. "Yes. The watch her father gave her. It is very powerful. Without it, the new cycle cannot begin."

The Timekeeper handed it over and said, "Only death can stop time."

Lady Fate held the watch carefully as she said in a low voice. "And cause the missing three seconds."

"Will you go see her?" The Timekeeper asked.

Lady Fate replied. "My time in Anglamora is done. Though I will see her again in another time and place."

The Timekeeper asked. "When?"

She replied. "I will come to her in ten Moderna years."

"What will they become...? The mystics of Anglamora?" He asked her.

Lady Fate looked directly at him before she replied. “They will become a book. A story told to children to inspire them to strive to be an inspiration. They too can be the eighth to stand between the light and darkness.”

“I will prepare the clocks and see you in ten years.” The Timekeeper said to Fate who nodded before she disappeared.

It took until only an hour before dark for the Anglamorian army and Evelyn Murray to make it to the border.

Once at the top of the mountain, Evelyn looked to the three horns. Max explained them to her. Evelyn requested King Darr to join her at the great horn. There she let the world know she had returned.

King Darr stood silent as Evelyn rubbed her hand on the great horn. She asked the druid if he was the one who blew it for her return. Before the druid could answer, someone else explained.

“Was me who blew the horn.” Destiny said to her.

Evelyn replied as she gave Destiny a hug. “I did not think I would see you again, Destiny.”

“The Fate, Karma and destiny of Anglamora is fulfilled. The destiny of Evelyn Murray is fulfilled. Yet, the destiny of two others is not.” Destiny said.

Evelyn replied. “I understand. I know what needs to be done and it will be.”

“I will see you in another time, Evelyn Murray.” Destiny said to her.

Just as the white haired girl started to walk away, she stopped and turned to face Evelyn one last time.

"Is not prideful or boastful to let the mystics of Anglamora know, the greatest mystic who ever lived has come home."

Everyone on that mountain heard what Destiny said and they all waited for Evelyn to respond.

King Darr said to her. "They find comfort in your power. They need to see it from time to time... I must admit. I too would like to see it once more."

Evelyn looked at Aerenthia who gave her a nod of approval. Likewise, the other six nodded to assure Evelyn she should make a statement using her mystique.

Evelyn turned to face the valley she loved above all other places. King Darr stepped up to the great horn. A few strands of Evelyn's hair began to rise as she lifted the white staff a few inches from the ground. Aerenthia and John smiled at each other as they took each other's hand.

King Darr blew hard into the great horn. Its magnitude caused ripples in the sea of the eastern shore of Danann that turned into a tsunami for Adierach.

The sound of the horn and its echo across the ice caused sudden volcanic eruptions in Moderna followed by many earthquakes. The ice wall in the northern prairie of Locklure gave way once again, and the stones of the black mountain shook.

Evelyn thumped her staff on the ground and a large white tornado formed at the southern end of the mountain she and her companions were on. The mystics of Anglamora gathered at the fire pit so they could see what was happening.

A small girl of around six years old pointed to the tornado and said, “Evelyn is home.”

Efely said not just to the girl but to everyone. “We don’t know if that is her or not.”

Evelyn Murray left no doubt. A large blue lightning bolt struck down from the cloudy sky into the center eye of the tornado. The top of the lightning bolt branched out in every direction like tree limbs across the sky.

Those on the mountain with her watched in wonder and admiration. Evelyn reached her left hand out and pushed downward. The tornado responded by collapsing. She turned her hand over with the palm up and slowly lifted her hand. The lightning bolt turned into a blue dome over Anglamora.

From the staff she cast a white light into the lightning bolt that flowed upward and turned the dome the same white starlight. Evelyn closed her hand and the dome exploded into silent rain drops of starlight. The white lightning bolt became a solid white tree like creation that would stand on the mountain for the Anglamorians to see for all time.

As the rain drops of white starlight fell, the little girl remarked. “That is Evelyn Murray.”

On the mountain, Evelyn said to King Darr, “Anglamora is home of the mystics. It is home to our friends in both the east and west.”

King Darr replied. “Danann will extend the same courtesy to Anglamora and Locklure. Together we will be the three powers of this realm.”

Evelyn and King Darr returned to the wagon. Once the old woman was seated, Darr took his place with his men. Osmo gave the order to march. Just before the wagon moved, Evelyn noticed John and Aerenthia were looking to her spot in the sky.

Evelyn put her hand on the armor of Aerenthia’s shoulder. Aerenthia turned to see Evelyn looking at that spot in the sky. While keeping her eyes to the sky, Evelyn assured Aerenthia of her legacy.

“From the air she came, to save us so many times... My friend, Lady Starlight.”

CHAPTER 14

Evelyn Murray was welcomed into Anglamora like a conquering queen. The children done what children do as they could not be patient. They swarmed the wagon once again. The smallest of them were carried by the older children and sat on Evelyn's lap. The older children were standing anywhere including dangling from the side of the wagon so they could touch her.

Evelyn tried her best to address each one by name and pass out hugs. The rest of the mystics lined the roadside and cheered while throwing flower peddles on Evelyn and the seven others beside her.

She looked around and noticed Christopher was not with the other children.

"Where has Christopher gone off to?" Evelyn asked Christina.

"I don't know. He was with us." She replied.

When the wagon approached the fire pit, Evelyn got her answer. Christopher had moved the chair by the door of her hut next to the pit. He was standing beside it with her old fireking cup in his hand.

"I think he has some tea for you." Christina told her.

Max stopped the wagon so Christopher was on his side.

"Sucking up already huh boy... What have you done now?" Max asked in a joking manner.

Mark helped Evelyn down and she went straight to Christopher. He held out the cup and Evelyn took it but not to drink. She sat the cup down on a stump and hugged him.

"I know you wanted to join the other children to come see me. You thinking of me first as I think of you first, is the greatest gift you could have given me." Evelyn said to him while holding him close to her.

All the children took advantage of Evelyn being out in the open. They surrounded her and held on tight.

The small girl climbed up Christina's back and Evelyn held onto her. The little girl began to cry as she said, "Please don't leave again."

"I won't Noari. I am home now for good." Evelyn assured Noari and the other children.

Slowly Evelyn was able to peel the children off her with the help of their parents. Only after she was free of the last child did she pick up her teacup.

Aerenthia still dressed in her armor made her way around the wagon in full view of the children and it was her turn to be surrounded.

Of course all the children referred to her as Lady Starlight and this time it made her uncomfortable.

Aerenthia pushed the children back just enough for her to squat down and look them in the eyes.

"I no longer have the power of starlight children. I am only a mortal woman now. So, I want you to call me Aerenthia instead of Lady Starlight... Okay."

Christopher said to her, "Aerenthia... From the air she came."

Christina followed where he left off. "Here in Anglamora, you will always be Lady Starlight to us."

Six year old Noari finished it along with Aerenthia's emotional reserve with the words of her innocent voice. "Anglamora's most beloved star."

The power of starlight was meaningless to the children. It was the love Aerenthia had always given to the Anglamorians that made her special.

Humility, the Mediator had said only a day before. It was the children of Anglamora who took fury away from Aerenthia and humbled Lady Starlight.

It was Aerenthia's war torn arms holding tight to the innocence of the children that humbled the men gathered around.

The moment was broken when Luke sat up in the back of the wagon. Upon seeing him, Christopher pointed at Luke and asked.

"Is he a prisoner? Did you do that to him Lady Starlight?"

Laughter immediately erupted from everyone standing at the pit. Even King Darr who rarely laughed out loud could not keep it contained.

Luke quickly said to Christopher, "Prisoner? I'll kick your ass!"

Luke had stiffened from the ride and the soreness of the battle settled in. He grunted and groaned as he tried to get out of the wagon.

Christopher laughed and continued. "You won't kick anything… You can't even get out of there."

Again, laughter followed his comment. Evelyn and Aerenthia thought it was especially funny.

"When I do get out of here, you better run." Luke replied to Christopher.

Evelyn put her final mark on being home when she scolded Christopher in her ornery way.

"Christopher, you little shit. Leave Luke alone before I turn you into a frog."

The children along with the mystics smiled. Then the children looked at Aerenthia as they waited for her to scold Evelyn. She did not disappoint.

"You shouldn't cuss Evelyn Murray. It's unbecoming." Aerenthia said with a wink.

At that point, for those who long dwelled in Anglamora, it was once again home.

Evelyn knew the men were tired and weak from the long battles and marches. She asked the mystics to prepare enough food for the soldiers and kings who accompanied her to Anglamora.

By this time, the darkness of night had settled in the valley, she asked the men of Danann to stay till morning. After such a long march from Locklure, there was no argument.

The candles in the houses of Anglamora once again burned, providing a faint light in the white forest. Yet so many were left still left dark. Thousands of men and women who fought beside them, dead. For Evelyn Murray it was very noticeable.

She fought through her emotions and told part of the story about her experience in death across the plane of time. Her tales of another existence did not last as she used her age as a way to excuse herself from the crowd. Just before she walked into the hut, she turned and looked directly at John Porter for a moment. John slightly nodded but did not say anything.

King Darr noticed and said to John. "You and the old one have a special bond. I can see that clearly. Words left unspoken. Unspoken words prevent the heart from healing."

John replied. "I love her as if she were my mother... And not long ago, I had to kill her. Even though she is back, I am still guilty."

Zethra was sitting on one side of King Darr at the other side of the table. She overheard and responded to John.

"Only in your mind are you guilty. Not to anyone else. You need to know that."

"Zethra is right my friend. You didn't kill her. You saved her." Osmo said to John as he nodded to Zethra.

Mark added. "You still don't see it do you? It was you who deemed her the eighth. You brought her out."

"You brought me out too John Porter." Erissa said to him.

Sanwren added. "You pulled me into the cemetery and saved me from burning alive. Let it go. Be free of it."

Aerenthia took John's hand and gave her advice. "You were left no choice. The things set in motion that day led to this day, and this was a good day. I believe she is expecting you to come talk to her."

"I know she is." John replied.

The children interrupted the conversation by gathering around staring at King Darr. Their presence did not go unnoticed.

"You may ask me anything." King Darr said.

Christopher asked. "Men refer to you as King. How can a boy like me become king?"

Everyone at the table grinned and waited for King Darr's response. The children were most attracted to King Darr's raspy voice. It was unlike anything they had ever heard from another child.

"I am old children, very old. I was not born in Danann. I came to Danann alone on a ship from far away. I am the keeper of the philosopher's stone. I found it when I was young and it has prevented me from showing my age."

Christina asked. "Would you like to age? Any at all?"

King Darr replied. "For many years I did. Not anymore. All that I have wanted to accomplish, I have in this appearance. So I ask, what is stopping any of you?"

While King Darr talked with the children, Aerenthia nudged John and motioned her head toward the hut. It was the perfect time for him to get away and John seized it.

John did not knock on Evelyn's door as it was one of her rules that no one did. Her door was always open to the Anglamorians.

John stepped inside the old hut and first noticed Karma's door was open. He paused for a moment as he listened to see if she was there.

"Get in here and sit down John Porter. Now that Karma is gone, Mark and Erissa will use that room." Evelyn said without looking at him.

John grinned and shook his head. It never ceased to amaze him how she could know such things.

He done what he was told and took a seat on the hearth of the fireplace so he could look directly at Evelyn who was sitting in her chair. She had a cup of wild mint tea prepared for him resting on the stump beside her. When he sat down, she handed it to him.

"You have suffered in some form since I have known you John Porter. Now it is time to let your heart heal. Our war is over. Let happiness replace the sadness and guilt."

John took a sip of his tea and replied. "What do I do now with no battle against the darkness to fight?"

Evelyn answered. "Live... Now you live John Porter."

John remained quiet while the old woman studied him. He repeatedly sipped his tea and his hands slightly shook. Evelyn could tell he was deeply troubled.

"Say it John Porter. Say what is hurting you so."

John said what she thought he would. "I never hurt so much as I did there by the lake. That creature watched with a smile while I killed the greatest person I have ever known. Worst of all, I couldn't do anything to stop it."

Evelyn replied. "Your words are too kind. One day I will be a memory and all that has happened will only be a dream. The greatest person you have ever known will still be by your side. You and Aerenthia deserve to be happy together after all this time."

John didn't reply right away. He sipped his tea and his mind wandered. Evelyn could tell he was still quite unsettled. She once again she tried to ease the pain in his heart.

"I won't forgive you John Porter for killing me... No sir, I will not. There is and never was anything to forgive. It is I who must ask your forgiveness. I accepted the terms. Here at the end of it all, I look back and believe it was the perfect plan."

John replied. "It did work out perfectly, I must admit. I guess I must find a way to forgive myself. I said I couldn't do it and I did. I was capable of it. I was capable of it without even being able to tell you that I loved you. I watched them all say it Evelyn... I watched them all give you a hug and I couldn't."

John's emotions were boiling inside him and his hands began to shake enough that he sat the cup down on the hearth. Evelyn leaned forward and took his hand in hers.

"I never seen a person so hurt as you were that day, John Porter. All that you felt, I felt as well. So now, let us be done with it. I could not hug you then, but I can now and I want to pay for it."

Evelyn turned John's hand over and from her left hand, she put the old wooden nickel in his palm. John immediately grinned as he saw it. Evelyn hugged him and patted him on the back as if he were a child. Though, all the Anglamorians were her children in her eyes.

"One of Aunt Katie's nickels... I always wanted one from her." John said.

Evelyn replied. "This was one of hers, not originally. I gave this very nickel to Katie Carpenter when she was a young girl. She laughed because the wooden nickel was useless. That is when I explained that it was priceless when used to purchase a hug from a friend or loved one. That is how it started John Porter."

Evelyn smiled at him before she poured the two of them another cup of tea. John tried to give the nickel back to Evelyn but she refused.

"One day there will be someone very special in your life. Someone young and innocent. That nickel is for a child who will come in your life many years from now."

John put the nickel in his pocket and took a drink of his tea before he changed the subject.

"I have a question about time for you mother."

Evelyn smiled and said, "You want to know about the missing three seconds."

John replied. "I do. I heard so much about it, and I was told it was a source of your power."

Evelyn explained. "When I was a small girl, I was struck by lightning... I died John Porter long before you killed me. I was dead for three seconds."

John couldn't figure it out. He asked. "Three seconds is not very long. How did that make any difference?"

Evelyn replied. "In death, time stops. Three seconds can be an eternity. For me, it was enough time to create the vortex of my time. It spins fast at the bottom and slow at the top. What seems like a day in Moderna can be years here in Anglamora. It is why the young never age and old never die. This plane across time is only one ring in the vortex. So for me as you all say, time doesn't count."

John asked. "How is it possible for such a young girl to even comprehend such a thing? I cannot fully comprehend it myself?"

Evelyn smiled and said, "This may trouble you further, but Katie Carpenter showed me how with an old watch."

John was shaking his head. He was completely lost and Evelyn knew it. She further explained.

"How was I the one who gave Katie the nickel when she was young while I was old? Yet she be the one who helped me when I was young and she was old? It is a loop in time. It is the cycle the three deities were so concerned about continuing.

"My father raised crops and mostly game foul. It was he who sent me out into the rain to gather eggs. After the lightning chose me for a target, it was my father who said I must have had another purpose to have survived. He taught me about the seven inspirations and said I could be the eighth. I wish he could have seen you John Porter, standing with the others when you deemed it so."

John said to her, "In my eyes you were always the eighth inspiration."

There was a pause between them both. Evelyn refilled their cups and they both sat quietly for a few seconds before John broke the silence.

"I want to marry Aerenthia, and I would very much like your blessing and for you to officiate the wedding if you would?"

Evelyn nodded and replied. "I would be honored John Porter."

John explained. "I want to take her to Moderna for a short time. I want to show her Katie's farm... The place you left to her. I want her to decide in which place we will live."

Evelyn let out a sigh and said, "You two will live in Moderna, John Porter. There you will tell the world about the Mystics of Anglamora. There you will start a new cycle. You must teach them, the people of that place, the position of the eighth is available to anyone who will accept it."

John grinned and jokingly asked. "What if Aerenthia says no when I ask her to marry me?"

Evelyn chuckled and said, “She doesn’t have the power of starlight anymore. I’ll kick her ass till she says yes.”

John laughed and shook his head at Evelyn. “You really are one ornery old woman you know that?”

Evelyn replied. “Well, it doesn't change anything John Porter.”

CHAPTER 15

Two days later under the moonlight at the northern side of the western mountain, Aerenthia did not say no.

The very next day, Max opened a gate for them to Moderna. Not just anywhere in the modern world of man, but in the yard of what was Evelyn's then Katie's farm.

It was the first time Aerenthia had put her feet on the ground in Moderna. The very first thing she asked was about an electric line. She could not imagine why there would be a line going to the house.

John explained its purpose. His explanation shocked her.

"Are all the homes in Moderna connected to this line? Do they communicate through it?"

John replied. "They talk through the bottom line. The top two make the lights come on."

"People should come speak to us directly. I think this line must go. How can one be free if we are dependent on such things and no privacy? No

John… This part of Moderna does not belong to us. We should not belong to it."

John and Aerenthia spent six days at the farm. The old farmhouse was still very clean as time moves differently in Anglamora. Katie had only been gone a short time from Moderna.

Aerenthia did like the tractor and how easy it was to plow. The riding lawnmower fascinated her. John showed her how it worked and Aerenthia gently rubbed her feet across the top of the grass. Mowing and plowing excited her and she was like a kid with a new toy playing on the yard equipment. She was uncomfortable with vehicles as she felt trapped inside. The seatbelt was not an option at all.

The house, though simple, she loved. John gave her a tour of the inside shocking her even more. Running water inside, hard wood floors instead of dirt and the toilet fascinated her. She flushed the toilet of the master bathroom several times. John thought it was funny as most people in Moderna would.

When they went in the kitchen, John rubbed his fingers on the old oak table before pulling a chair back to sit down. Aerenthia sat down across from him.

"This table belonged to my uncle Tom Carpenter. You would not believe the conversations that have taken place here between Evelyn and Tom."

From the table, John looked out the kitchen window just above the white porcelain sink. He was very nervous of what Aerenthia thought about the place.

She calmed him when she said, “This is a good place. It’s peaceful and private here.”

“Could you live here Aerenthia? Or would you rather live in Anglamora?” John asked.

Aerenthia replied. “I love Anglamora, but we are not needed there anymore. I think here is where we begin again.”

“You’re right Aerenthia… It is quiet here. Too quiet. I think some roosters crowing would help it feel like a home.” John said as she slowly nodded.

Aerenthia added. “A child for me would be what makes it a home. I have loved the children of Anglamora from the first day I saw them. From that day to now I have longed for my own.”

John replied. “I can think of no one who would be a better mother than you.”

Aerenthia asked. “You do know the rules of Anglamora?”

John replied. “I do. If the child is born outside of Anglamora, the parents can never again return. Have you ever wondered why Aerenthia? Why such a rule was made?”

She replied. “Like Anglamora, children are innocent. They must discover Anglamora on their own. They must answer the call of the mystics without interference.”

"Hopefully one day, Evelyn will come to our child and let them experience the magic of Anglamora." John said to her.

Aerenthia said, "I do not think she would be able to resist. After all, Evelyn Murray as you know is everyone's mother."

"Do we tell the child our story Aerenthia, or leave it secret?" John asked.

Aerenthia replied. "I do not think we should decide this right now. We are not even married yet."

John nodded and sat quietly for a moment with his thoughts. Aerenthia let him think as she sat quietly with thoughts of her own.

However, the silence didn't last. Aerenthia said to him, "We must go back for now... I think you know that. It will take time to transition from Anglamora to Moderna."

John replied. "I couldn't agree more. I miss them so much already. We will have to slowly start spending more time here until we get over the home sickness of Anglamora. Then we will be ready."

Before the dark of night fell on Moderna, John and Aerenthia went into the woods one hundred yards to the east of the farmhouse. They walked down a trail hand in hand until they came to a single post with a revolving gate.

The gate of handmade wooden planks was on the right side of the post when they faced it. John pulled the gate toward himself and moved it around to the left side of the post. When he pulled the gate open, it revealed the white forest of Anglamora.

John and Aerenthia were at the edge of the forest and prairie along the creek that flowed from beside Evelyn's hut.

When John let go of the gate, on the Moderna side, it swung back to its resting position on the right side of the post.

At the first sight of John and Aerenthia on the cobblestone road, the announcement of their return was said loudly at the firepit. Those sitting stood up, and the those standing turned to see them.

Christopher took off running to meet them as if they had been gone a long time. He was very excited as he grabbed Aerenthia's hand and demanded they hurry.

"Come on Lady Starlight! You won't believe who has come to see Evelyn."

John and Aerenthia ran behind Christopher to see what the commotion was about. Aerenthia got to Evelyn first and immediately stopped and smiled. John couldn't see what was going on.

He took enough time to nod to the other men and women gathered around.

"You won't believe your own eyes." Osmo said to John in a low voice.

John made it to where Evelyn was sitting in her chair next to the firepit. He stopped and looked shocked as his eyes grew wide.

Evelyn said to John. "These are the Capimalli John Porter. Long ago, I planted the old oak from whence they came."

Osmo was right. The sight of the Capimalli was unbelievable. They were a small tribe of tree spirits. Their heads and bodies were acorns. Their legs and arms were twigs from the old oak tree. Some were bearded with moss and others had usnea hair. They were led by their chief Graystone. The Capimalli only stood on average two inches tall. All ten that had come to see Evelyn were standing on a stump in front of her.

Evelyn introduced John as she pointed to the leader who had a long usnea beard.

"This is Chief Graystone, the leader of the Capimalli. Like me, he is the oldest of them all. He was the first from the tree, and he has brought these young ones on a journey to learn about the forest and to see me." Evelyn explained.

Aerenthia took John's hand and pulled him down to his knees with her.

Aerenthia said to Chief Graystone, "I am no longer starlight my old friend. I am only a woman now. I must apologize for not shinning a light on the old oak. Please do not think less of me."

The chief pointed his little staff toward Evelyn's staff. Evelyn let her staff down so the crystal was close to him.

Chief Graystone spoke in the voice of an old man that was magnified by the staff so everyone could hear.

"Stand." The chief demanded as he pointed his hand at Aerenthia.

She done what he asked and stood up straight. All who were gathered around moved in close to try to see the Capimalli leader who continued.

"From the air she came to guide our keeper to safety. In the absence of moonlight, she cast her own to keep us safe. From the sky or from the ground she is the same."

Graystone turned to his pupils and continued. "She is Aerenthia, and she will always be our most beloved star."

After his speech, Chief Graystone kneeled and lowered his head to Aerenthia. His pupils immediately followed. The Anglamorians did not value themselves above the Capimalli. Line after line, the men and women of Anglamora kneeled.

Evelyn looked up at Aerenthia who stood alone and winked at her as she nodded her head. The innocence and respect shown by the Capimalli meant the world to Aerenthia.

When the Anglamorians and Capimalli stood, Evelyn said to all who were there.

"The Mediator said humility was the eighth inspiration. I think he is wrong. To some he may be right. To some of you I might be in your eyes the eighth inspiration."

Everyone nodded in agreement that Evelyn was the eighth. To Evelyn it was someone different.

Evelyn continued. "To be a light in someone else's darkness, I believe is the eight inspiration."

Evelyn looked in the eyes of Aerenthia who was tearful and slightly shaking her head no. Evelyn nodded at her before she continued.

"Lady Starlight has always been that inspiration for me. Chief Graystone of the Capimalli agrees. Be a guiding light is what the old oaks say."

Aerenthia replied with a broken voice. "Thank you all for the kind words but it is more than I deserve."

Zethra said to Aerenthia, "It's your humble heart that seals it."

Osmo changed the mood into laughter when he commented.

"Humble, kind, and all those things we should long to be… Until she gets mad. I hope you remember her other name when you two get into an argument John… What happened to John Porter? Oh you didn't hear?"

All but Aerenthia laughed. She gave Osmo a dirty look with a slight grin as she shook her head which made it even funnier.

John's laughter slowly faded away even as the men kept telling jokes. He knew his time of being there and seeing all of them would one day end. He looked at Evelyn Murray and she could see it in his eyes.

"There is no hurry John Porter." She said to him.

John nodded but didn't say anything. Evelyn looked at the Capimalli and then back to John before she suggested.

"The Capimalli have been on a long journey. They would like to see the wedding. Could we have it tomorrow evening?"

John's eyes grew wide as it was very sudden. Before he could speak, Aerenthia answered.

"Tomorrow evening would be perfect. That is unless John objects."

Her words brought more laughter from Osmo and the men.

"You better not object John if you know what's good for you." Theodess yelled out.

John stood up and took Aerenthia's hands before he replied.

"We have waited through death and pain. I do not want to wait anymore."

"So be it." Evelyn said as she began to get up out of her chair.

Evelyn took off toward her hut and Max gathered the Capimalli in his hands to take inside with her.

John joined the other men to take the jokes they had coming. The women of Anglamora surrounded Aerenthia and took her with them across the creek to Efely's stump house to prepare.

Inside the hut, Max sat the Capimalli down on the left side of the fireplace hearth where they would be safe from the fire. Evelyn began pulling leaves off dried plants hanging from her ceiling.

"You know the rules of Anglamora Max. Rules we all agreed to many years ago." Evelyn said in a wondering tone.

Max replied. "About a child."

"Yes. If the child is born outside of Anglamora the parents can never again return." Evelyn continued.

Max asked. "What's on your mind Evelyn?"

"John and Aerenthia will have a child in Moderna. Can you make that gate only open for the child or would we have to go directly?" Evelyn asked him.

Max replied. "I have never made a gate for a single person, but I can try to make it work."

Evelyn put the leaves in the smoke blackened pot and moved it over the fire before she sat down. Her silence was deafening to Max.

He suggested. "I sense there is something very special about the child? Is there, Evelyn?"

Evelyn let out a sigh and said, "There is no star to guide the child here. The gate must remain."

"It will... Just like your secrets mother." Max replied.

Evelyn grinned and said in a low voice. "You will know in the end."

CHAPTER 16

Daylight the next morning came fast. Too fast for those who celebrated the night before, and not fast enough for John and Aerenthia.

Their wedding drew an audience from the three realms. John, Aerenthia and Evelyn Murray stood on the high bank of the lake in the prairie of Anglamora. The Capimalli stood five at each side on Evelyn's shoulders. King Eshnar and the druids of Locklure looked on from the top of the western mountain.

King Darr stood beside Old Toby and a company of his men who fought alongside them at the ice wall. It was the first time many had ever witnessed, King Darr was fully dressed in white armor instead of just a loin cloth.

The Anglamorians gathered along the base of the bank and looked on. Efely had made a new dress for Aerenthia that wasn't white as all the others. This one was sky blue with silver lace lining and a high collar that reached the back of her head.

John Porter like always was dressed in black leather. The silver buttons of his corset shinned against the sunlight and the polished leather duster glistened as he moved.

To the people of the second earth within the ice rings, they were a beautiful sight. A sight that would seem quite odd in Moderna. Moderna being the place they would fit in the least, yet believed it was the place of their future.

The marriage of John and Aerenthia was the final chapter in the quest for peace in Anglamora. For Evelyn Murray, it meant a new beginning.

At the end of the ceremony, John hugged Evelyn and thanked her and Aerenthia followed.

Evelyn said to them, "This is your day. Enjoy every minute of it with your friends."

John and Aerenthia glanced at each other as they knew she was referring to their limited time in Anglamora.

King Darr was first to shake hands with John Porter at the bottom of the embankment.

"The man who become the Grim who became an inspiration, John Porter... My friend." Said King Darr.

John replied. "To be a friend of King Darr is a great honor. We are all blessed to know you."

The King continued. "Should you decide to stay in Anglamora, Danann will always welcome you as one of our own and a friend."

Aerenthia responded. "The war is over in this realm my good friend, King Darr. That same evil plagues Moderna. It is where we are needed most."

King Darr bowed his head to Aerenthia and remained silent. King Lundar of Danann's eastern shore was next to shake hands and speak to the newlyweds.

"What a wild ride it has been since we first met."

John smiled as he raised his eyebrows and nodded his head.

"A wild ride is putting it lightly King Lundar. Yet here we are after all this time. I couldn't have made it without your help and leadership. I don't think any of us could have."

King Lundar replied. "It was an honor to serve Anglamora. An even greater honor to stand beside you both in battle."

Osmo and Theodess stepped in from behind Lundar and both wrapped their arms around John and the King.

Osmo said Jokingly. "Do we cry now or cry later?"

The men laughed and Zethra took Aerenthia by the hand.

"Let me save you from these savages." Zethra said as she smiled at the men.

Lundar, Theodess and Osmo dragged John to a larger group of men where Luke was sitting on a stump next to a wine barrel with cup in hand.

"Done got yourself hitched John Porter. You won't be worth a damn for sure now." Luke said jokingly.

Mark said to Luke. "Osmo and I are married."

Luke looked at Sanwren and grinned as he said, "See what I mean."

After that it was a free for all with the jokes among the men.

Zethra, Erissa, Efely and many of the other women were standing with Aerenthia at a long table covered in food.

"Seeing this day come makes all the turmoil of the past worth it. Wouldn't you agree Aerenthia?" Zethra asked.

Aerenthia replied. "It was worth it before this day."

Erissa changed the subject. "Efely this dress you made for Aerenthia is gorgeous. I love it."

Efely replied. "Thank you. I knew it had to be special. As special as I could possibly make it for the wedding day of Lady Starlight."

"Please call me Aerenthia... I am not Lady Starlight anymore." Aerenthia demanded.

Efely responded. "As long as you are my friend, here in Anglamora, I will call you Lady Starlight unless it really bothers you that much."

Aerenthia replied. "It does not bother me. It is just not true anymore."

Efely took Aerenthia's right hand in hers as she said, "It is to me."

Aerenthia hugged Efely and immediately demanded they eat. As the ladies began to set down, Aerenthia asked.

"Where is Evelyn?"

Zethra replied as she pointed her hand toward the cobblestone road.

"It looks like she is returning to her hut. Could be too much excitement for her."

Erissa replied. "That's not it. She feels that pieces of herself are missing. None of us have paid the price she has. We lost friends and loved ones in the war while Evelyn Murray lost children. She is without her close friends Karma, Destiny, Fate, Katie Carpenter, most of the reapers and soon Lady Starlight. She feels alone in a sea of faces."

Aerenthia had a very serious look on her face as she looked at Erissa. Aerenthia pushed her plate away before she replied to Erissa.

"She is not alone. Nor is she without starlight."

Aerenthia stood up and left the table. She stood out like a single star on a dark night as she walked through the crowd toward the road.

Efely said as she kept her watery eyes fixed on Aerenthia. "That is why I will always call her Lady Starlight."

John noticed Aerenthia going toward the road to join Evelyn. He stood up but Mark grabbed his duster at the same time Aerenthia shook her head no to him.

Mark told John. "You had your moment with mother. Let Aerenthia have hers."

John asked. "Evelyn is walking as if she is sad. Is she okay?"

Max replied to John in Destiny's way of speaking. "Is a heavy price to pay to be Evelyn Murray."

John asked. "Did Destiny tell you that?"

Max replied. "Many times."

Mark explained. "All those lost in the war against Luciftias were her children... At least in her eyes they were. She is the last of the great powers now that Karma, Destiny, Fate and Katie Carpenter are gone. Soon she will be without Lady Starlight. I think that hurts her most."

John immediately replied. "Then we won't stay in Moderna."

John's heart broke all over again as his mind went back to the lakeshore at Locklure.

"I can't hurt her again." John said with terrible sadness to Mark.

It was the first time the men of Anglamora saw how big the scar was on John's heart. None of them knew what to say to him. They just watched him in silence as he watched Aerenthia and Evelyn fade from sight within the white forest.

Leave it to Luke to have no reserve. "Quit acting like a little girl John Porter."

John quickly looked at Luke as if he were ready to fight. Everyone around who heard it was silent.

Luke continued. "You're holding onto an unwarranted emotion. That's what young girls do. I mean what more can you ask for? I wasn't destined to become the Grim. It wasn't my destiny to follow that order to set Luciftias up for defeat. Mother knew what she was doing, and it worked. It worked because your love for Aerenthia was strong enough to keep you alive to fulfill that order. Otherwise, you would have refused and died too. Then there would not have been eight in the end. Not the right eight anyway. So what more do you want? We all fought the war John Porter, but you won it for everyone. So quit your complaining and self pity."

Sanwren added. "He's right John. It was a great destiny."

John let out a sigh and replied. "Yeah I know he's right. Let's just not tell him that very much or he will start thinking we need to listen to him."

John's response brought a smile from most and a nod from Luke. John took his cup to the wine barrel to fill it before he sat down on a stump next to Luke.

The two men shook hands and John thanked Luke for his bold honesty.

Aerenthia had caught up to Evelyn just before the firepit in front of her hut. Evelyn sat the Capimalli down on the ground at the edge of the wood line on the creek side. Chief Graystone and his pupils bowed their heads to Evelyn before they began their long journey back to the great oak at the northeast corner of Anglamora.

Evelyn used the white staff to help herself up. She watched the Capimalli began their journey as she said to Aerenthia who was behind her.

"A journey that would take us only two days will take them a month as a clock turns in Moderna. I offered to see them returned safe, but Chief Graystone refused. It is the journey that makes the memories he said to me."

"I'm not sure we should live in Moderna Evelyn." Aerenthia said to her.

Evelyn replied. "You are greatly mistaken in your reasoning my friend, Aerenthia."

"Am I?" Aerenthia asked.

"Yes, you are. You question it on my behalf. However, on my behalf you must." Evelyn said.

Aerenthia demanded. "Quit speaking in parables Evelyn Murray. What is it you are saying?"

Evelyn Explained. "You and John are the only two here in this land today who still have a destiny to fulfill. If you stay in Anglamora, it will be left undone... All will be undone.

"You two must begin spending more time in Moderna. Slowly over time, you will be visitors to the mystics instead of one of us. It will make the transition much easier."

Aerenthia said. "John and I have talked about that and agree. Until then we do not want to leave anything undone or unsaid here. All the old wounds must be healed."

Evelyn replied. "And they will be Aerenthia. Not all in one day or even one week. Nor must it be done so hastily."

Evelyn stood beside Aerenthia, put her hand on Aerenthia's back before she continued.

"You're very special to me Lady Starlight. It does sadden me that a day will come when you will no longer walk in this valley just as it saddens you. I have told and you know that you were always my guiding light. You always were and always will be."

Aerenthia wrapped an arm around Evelyn as they both watched the creek flow over the white stones at the bottom.

Aerenthia replied. "You were always my eighth inspiration. Your story is the one that must be told in Moderna. John is going to write a book based on all that has happened here. I think he told you."

Evelyn answered. "Yes, he did tell me that."

Aerenthia continued. "We talked about having a child. We know the rules of Anglamora if the child is not born here. I ask, please leave the gate standing for that child to one day walk in this valley."

Evelyn grinned and stepped around so she could look at Aerenthia.

Evelyn replied. "That has already been decided by myself and Max. Since you mention the gate, I remember a gate from my childhood that was much like the one you speak of. My mother use to tell me to leave it alone but I was drawn to it."

Aerenthia's eyes wandered about and she grew a confused look before she asked.

"You have never spoken about your mother to me before. Tell me about her, please."

Evelyn done what she asked. "You remind me of her Aerenthia, so much you do. She was an incredible woman who told tales of far away places. She described them as if she were looking down on them from a high place. Like an angel looking down from heaven.

"She supported my father in all he ventured to do, and they would look at each other as if they had great adventures and tales they would not share with me. I never pushed the subject as I let them keep their secrets.

"There were no animals either on the farm or wild that would not come to her. She brought everything to life wherever she went. Sometimes at night, she would stand in the yard and look up at the night sky. Seems like I remember the stars cast a special glow around her.

"Mother is God in the eyes of a child Aerenthia. My mother was to me when I was young. She was sunshine on stormy days and starlight on dark moon nights. It was her who eventually told me it was time to open that old gate. I think she knew when I crossed to the other side, she would never see me again."

Aerenthia asked. "I know your mystical powers. Did you ever go look for them?"

Evelyn replied. "Yes... Across the plane of time, I could see them, but they could not see me. Although, I left clues for them, and they knew I had been there. My parents understood it Aerenthia. They were the first to tell me, I would one day be the most powerful mystic to ever live. After that, with the help of few deities, the cycle was formed."

"Anyway, shouldn't you and John be together enjoying today instead of you being here listening to the ramblings of an old woman?"

Aerenthia replied. "He and I will have many years together. My time here with you is numbered. With that said, why are we not having a hot cup of tea?"

With a smile and hug, the two of them started toward the hut. The ramblings of Evelyn Murray continued.

"My father liked wild mint tea... My mother not so much but she would drink it with me."

Aerenthia opened the door for Evelyn and shut it behind them. Once the door was shut, Destiny appeared next to the firepit looking at Evelyn's hut.

"Don't tell her too much Evelyn Murray." Destiny said in a low voice just before she once again disappeared.

CHAPTER 17

Aerenthia and John Porter done exactly as they planned. Their visits to Moderna slowly became stays and their stays in Anglamora changed to visits. It was a process that took almost two years.

The last year they only visited Anglamora twice. Once was to announce that Aerenthia was with child, and the next visit would be their last. It was a visit with Evelyn Murray and the children of Anglamora.

John and Aerenthia had slowly transformed into regular looking people of Moderna. Aerenthia still wore mostly dresses but not anything like the handmade dresses Efely made. Around the house she grew accustomed to jeans, although they seemed odd to her. She even began to wear shoes. Running shoes being her favorite for daily use.

John Porter had changed from his usual black clothing to blue jeans, slip on boots, and usually a black shirt. In Moderna they looked normal, but in Anglamora they looked odd.

John and Aerenthia stood at the gate in the woods east of their house. They paused and looked at each other as they knew it would be the last time they would step through. Aerenthia's stomach bulge from her pregnancy was easy to see.

"It's early morning there Aerenthia. We need to get in and get out before the Anglamorians gather. Otherwise, we will be there all day, and this is going to hard enough the way it is." John said to her as stepped up to the gate.

John was holding a book in his left hand as he used his right hand to swing the gate around and then open it. This time it did not lead them to the forest edge at the prairie, but to the firepit.

Morning in Anglamora meant the children had gathered for learning from Evelyn Murray. Christopher was the first to notice their arrival.

"John and Lady Starlight are here!" He shouted with excitement.

The children ran to gather around their guests and to welcome them with hugs. Each of the children had to get a good look at Aerenthia's stomach.

Young Noari put her tiny hand on Aerenthia's belly and asked. "Will your baby be starlight too?"

Aerenthia replied. "Yes Noari... As all children are."

Christopher and Christina were old enough to understand. They give a quick smile and nod but remained silent. John picked Noari up as he began toward Evelyn.

"We have to say hi to Evelyn too." John told Noari

She held tight around John's neck as if she knew it was the last time he would hold her. Even when he sat down on a stump, Noari held onto him.

"Let him go Noari and take a seat of your own." Evelyn said to the little girl.

John sat Noari on his left knee and said, "She can sit right here for a few minutes."

Noari stuck her tongue out at Evelyn who immediately responded.

"You think you got away with something don't you? You little shit. Where's my stick?"

The other children smiled and shook their heads at Evelyn before they looked at Aerenthia who scolded her.

"You shouldn't cuss Evelyn Murray… It's unbecoming."

In that moment, for the children, Anglamora had come full circle. It was the normality they long desired.

Evelyn replied in her usual ornery way. "Well, it doesn't change anything. It's what they are."

"No we're not!" Noari exclaimed to Evelyn.

John asked Noari. "Not even a little bit?"

Noari smiled and replied. "Maybe a little sometimes."

"Precious is what the children are." A familiar long unheard voice said from behind them. Destiny had returned to Anglamora.

"Wisteria is here!" Noari shouted.

John added. “Yes she is after all this time.”

At six years old, no one explained to Noari that Wisteria was Destiny or how significant she was. Noari knew her only as a friend called by two names.

Destiny hugged Evelyn first before she turned her sights to Aerenthia who was sitting in a wooden chair. The children stepped to the side to make way for Destiny.

Not a word was spoken as Destiny knelt down and put her hand on Aerenthia’s belly. Destiny looked directly at Aerenthia before she spoke.

“All children are starlight. The one you carry will be a great beacon of light in the dark places of the world. Yes... She is starlight indeed.”

The children immediately began whispering to each other, “It’s a girl.”

“Yes, it is going to be a girl.” John said to the children.

Destiny looked at John with a smile and a nod of respect and appreciation.

John asked. “What do we owe to be blessed by a visit from Destiny?”

“Debts are paid John Porter. Was a heavy price to pay.” Destiny replied.

John sat Noari down so he could stand up. Destiny took his hand in hers as she looked up at him.

“A love like Evelyn’s is taught, John Porter. It is taught through love. If you teach it to her, she will see anything other than love as darkness. If you teach it through example, she will strive to be a light in the darkness of others so they too may experience it."

Destiny looked at Aerenthia as she followed up.

"She will be starlight, an inspiration to all."

Upon her words, Destiny disappeared. Silence followed among those at the firepit. Evelyn sat with a grin as she seemed to be admiring John and Aerenthia.

Christopher said, "She use to seem strange to me when she was Wisteria. Now I think she is magnificent."

Christina replied to Christopher. "Everyone thinks you're strange Chris."

Christopher smiled and said, "I might be but at least I don't look like you."

Christopher and Christina began shoving and wrestling each other until Evelyn stopped it.

"If you two don't stop that bickering, I will tell people you're in love with each other." Evelyn said as she winked at John.

"Ewe!" Christina remarked as she quit fighting.

Christopher added. "That's gross Evelyn."

"You're gross!" Christina said to Christopher.

Evelyn shook her head and demanded, "You kids get out of here and go play or go home for a little while. I want to talk to John and Aerenthia alone."

Noari said. "But they just got here."

Evelyn ordered the children to give John and Aerenthia a hug and go back to their homes so the three of them could speak. One by one each of the children gave a hug and said goodbye. Only John and Aerenthia knew it would be for the last time.

When the children crossed the creek, John handed his book to Evelyn Murray.

"I finally finished it." He said as he nervously watched her. Evelyn carefully rubbed her hand over the leather binding as she read the title out loud.

"The Three Powers by John Porter. Tell me John Porter. What do you consider the three powers to be?" Evelyn asked.

John replied. "Here in Anglamora for many years, you and Aerenthia were the two great powers. It might sound bad to say but Luciftias was the third. So, for me, it was this."

John pointed his hand to Aerenthia and said, "The power of light is one. Luciftias was the power of darkness. You mother was and still are the power to choose. The power to choose being the most powerful of them all."

Evelyn was pleased with his answer. She replied. "That has been what I have tried to teach for all these years."

"I want you to have that copy. I had it custom made just for you. None of the others are leather bound and hand pressed. It is a book designed for the Anglamorians and no others."

Evelyn opened it and read the inside of the cover. She smiled and closed the book as she held it close to her chest.

"I will cherish this gift just as I have cherished our friendships. With this book being done and Aerenthia with child, I suspect this is the last time I will see you two."

Aerenthia responded with tearful eyes. "Yes, you are correct. I want you to know Evelyn, I did the best I could to be a friend and service to you."

Evelyn replied. "It has never been done better, my friend Lady Starlight."

Evelyn got up and sat the book down in her chair. Aerenthia stood up and the two hugged each other as best friends parting ways on good terms.

John was next to get a hug from Evelyn as she said to him, "It has been a great honor to know you, to call you my friend and to love you as a son."

"You said it Evelyn... It has never been done better. As a mother and a friend to all of us, you set the bar high."

The mystics of Anglamora were beginning to stir and move toward the firepit.

Evelyn said to John and Aerenthia. "If you two don't want to be stuck here saying goodbye all day, you better go now."

John said to Evelyn. "I love you Evelyn and thank you for everything you've done."

Evelyn was holding back her emotions even as her eyes began to water.

She replied. "I love you both. Your legend will live on here with the mystics."

John and Aerenthia walked to the open gate where the woods of their property could be seen on the other side. The mystics had closed in around the firepit and began waving and shouting their love for John and Lady Starlight.

They were all there gathered around. Theodess, Osmo and Zethra along with Efely and the children who ran back across the creek to see them off. Mark and Erissa waved from the door of the hut. All the mystics looked on as Aerenthia returned what Evelyn had done for her so many times.

Aerenthia pointed to Evelyn and shouted so all could hear her.

"She is Evelyn Murray! The greatest mystic who ever lived!"

Aerenthia stood tall and kept her reserve while John waved to his friends as he shut the gate for the last time. As soon as John swung the gate back to its right position, Aerenthia put her head on his chest and wept.

They knew the departure would not be easy. However, imagining something is much different that experiencing it. Before walking back to their house, Aerenthia broke John's embrace so she could rub the gate with her hand.

One month later their daughter was born. At the first sight of her eyes, both John and Aerenthia noticed a small bright white dot in her pupils. She was starlight just as Destiny had said she would be.

A nurse in the room asked if they had picked a name for the girl. John and Aerenthia both replied at the same time with the name, Evelyn.

The nurse said, "That's not a very common name anymore."

John replied. "It will be."

Aerenthia added. "Evelyn Starlight Porter will be her name."

The nurse replied. "That's perfect given the spots on her eyes."

"The name does not come from the spots on her eyes... It is a destiny." Aerenthia said just before the nurse left the room.

CHAPTER 18

Eight years and one day shy of one month had passed since John and Aerenthia last looked upon Anglamora. Young Evelyn had grew to be a very curious, mischievous and intelligent little girl.

John was sitting at the old oak table drinking coffee while Aerenthia made breakfast when Evelyn walked into the kitchen rubbing her eyes.

"Look who's awake." John said to Aerenthia.

Evelyn climbed onto John's lap while she was still trying to wake up.

Aerenthia asked. "Did you sleep well?"

Evelyn shook her head yes and replied. "I had a dream. There were seven people waiting for me. They kept yelling my name, but I couldn't get to them."

"Is that what woke you up?" Aerenthia asked.

Evelyn nodded and John said to them, "It's probably from the story I told you about the seven inspirations who stood between the light and darkness. Do you think that might be what it is?"

Evelyn sat up straight and said, "Probably."

Rain began to pour outside with a few claps of thunder in the distance.

Evelyn asked. “Dad, will you feed and water the birds since it’s raining?”

John replied. “You know the rule. If you don’t feed them, you don’t eat. You should have gotten up earlier instead of sleeping in. It’s your chore. Your mom and I have our own.”

Evelyn replied. “Maybe the rain will stop in a little bit. I’ll feed those little shits then.”

Aerenthia immediately turned around and said, “I don’t want to hear you say that word again. You shouldn’t cuss Evelyn... It’s unbecoming.”

Aerenthia covered her own mouth and began to tear up as she turned back around to face the stove.

John noticed and continued with scolding Evelyn. “You know you are not supposed to talk like that Evelyn.”

Evelyn replied. “I’m sorry I said it, but it doesn’t change anything. It’s what they are.”

Aerenthia stopped moving and stood still. John pointed to a wooden basket by the door before he demanded.

“That may be Evelyn. Now get your raincoat on and take your basket to gather eggs while you’re out there. If you get it over with it’s done. This rain is supposed to get worse as the day goes on so do it now.”

She asked. “Since tomorrow is my birthday, will I have to do it then too?”

John replied. "I guess since it is your birthday tomorrow, I will take care of them for you."

John's reply made Evelyn happy and it showed in her demeanor. She got dressed and put her rain coat on to do her morning chores. John and Aerenthia were waiting for her to go outside so they could talk. Once young Evelyn walked outside, Aerenthia said what she was thinking.

"The closer it has gotten to her eight birthday, the more she says things like Evelyn Murray. Have you noticed?"

John replied. "Of course I have. It's why I told her the story about the seven inspirations. I wanted to see what she would say."

Aerenthia asked. "Last night when you told her that story, did she ask you why there wasn't eight?"

"No she didn't. She said it was good story and went to sleep." John told her.

Aerenthia turned around to face John before she continued.

"Evelyn Murray spoke in parables quite often. I do not. So I'm just going to say it. Are we expecting her to be Evelyn Murray? Have we led her to act this way?"

John replied. "I don't think so. We have never mentioned Evelyn's name to her. Nor have we influenced her by using some of Evelyn Murray's sayings. Whatever is going on, it is not us doing it."

Both of them stayed silent for just a moment as their minds wondered through many thoughts. In a sudden, John's eyes grew wide.

"She once told me she got struck by lightning the day before her eighth birthday." John said as he stood up and started toward the door.

"Get her in here John. Get her right now!" Aerenthia demanded.

Before John could say anything, a loud explosion sounded from a lightning strike. Aerenthia screamed as she looked through the kitchen window. John took off outside across the yard to Evelyn's lifeless body lying in the yard.

Three seconds it was from the time the lightning hit, till John Porter first put his hands on Evelyn. Upon his touch, she took a deep breath and opened her eyes very wide. Her clothes were burnt in several places and were still smoking when John picked her up.

"What happened?" Evelyn asked with a distressed voice before she started crying.

John was rushing her to the house when he answered. "You were hit by lightning."

Aerenthia met them at the door and grabbed Evelyn's hand, staying with her as John walked to the couch to lay her down.

John and Aerenthia's nervous excitement was scaring Evelyn more than the storm.

"We have to get her clothes off. The electric had to leave somewhere. Aerenthia take her shoes off. Check her feet." John demanded.

Without hesitation, Aerenthia done what he asked and found no evidence of electrocution. Evelyn began telling them she was fine. She didn't feel like she was hurt. John wasn't taking any chances. He checked her stomach, mainly around the naval cavity and then rolled her over to check her back.

"Take her in the bathroom Aerenthia and check her from head to toe." John demanded.

Evelyn exclaimed. "I am okay. I'm not hurting anywhere."

Her words fell on deaf ears. Aerenthia scooped her up in her arms and started toward the hall to her bedroom.

"I can walk mom. You don't have to carry me." Evelyn said still trying to convince them she was okay.

John was still on his knees at the couch and shaking all over. He finally got to his feet only to anxiously wait to hear from Aerenthia.

Only a few minutes passed by until Evelyn and Aerenthia walked back to the kitchen. Evelyn had a different pair of clothes on. Aerenthia tossed the burnt clothes in the trash.

"I can't find anything wrong with her John." Aerenthia said as she shrugged her shoulders.

John picked up Evelyn and nearly hugged the life out of her. He sat down at the table with Evelyn on his knee. There he began to apologize for sending her out in the storm.

"You don't need to be sorry dad... Sometimes I forget how much they depend on me. They can't feed themselves." Evelyn said trying to take the self blame away from her dad.

John eased up on his bear hug and told her he would go make sure the game fowl were okay. He instructed her to stay inside when opened the door to go do her chores.

Aerenthia made a plate for Evelyn but stopped before giving it to her.

"Do you feel like eating baby girl? That was quite an ordeal." Aerenthia asked.

Evelyn replied. "I'm starving. It feels like I haven't eaten in days."

Aerenthia gave her the plate, then walked to the other side of the house to her room and got the old watch out from John's nightstand.

It was the watch the Timekeeper had given to John in the box canyon west of Locklure. Aerenthia opened the pocket watch and seen that it was working fine. She carried it into the kitchen and put it on the table close by Evelyn but didn't say anything.

It didn't take long for young Evelyn to pick it up and look at it. She quickly sat it back down and continued eating.

Aerenthia asked. "What time is it Evelyn?"

The girl replied. "I'll have to check the clock in the living room."

Aerenthia asked. "What's wrong with the time on that old watch?"

Evelyn replied. "It doesn't work. It's stuck."

Aerenthia walked over and stood where she could see. Evelyn held up the watch in her hand and said, "See."

Aerenthia did see. The second hand was bouncing.

"I guess you are right. It doesn't work anymore." Aerenthia said as she took the watch from Evelyn.

In Aerenthia's hand it worked fine. At that moment, she knew the new cycle had begun. It was at this point she understood the rule of Anglamora about parents. It would have to be her secret until later that night after Evelyn had gone to bed.

That night when John got out of the shower, he looked through his open bedroom door but didn't see Aerenthia in the living area. There were no sounds coming from inside the house suggesting she was in there. John walked to the window of his bedroom and pulled back the curtain. Aerenthia was outside in the yard looking up at the night sky.

He quietly joined Aerenthia in the yard and looked up toward the stars beginning to shine as the storm clouds faded away.

"I thought you may come out here tonight after the events of today." John said to her.

Aerenthia replied. "The lightning was not the only event. I handed the watch to Evelyn and it stopped working. We are raising Evelyn Murray."

John thought about what she said for a moment before he gave his own thoughts.

"It is how she described it. Exactly for that matter. I really think that Evelyn Murray and our daughter are not the same person to be perfectly honest Aerenthia."

Aerenthia looked at John and asked. "How can that be given what we know?"

John took a deep breath and let it out slowly before he continued.

"Remember what the Mediator said? He told Evelyn Murray that Luciftias didn't exist, and all things have an equal. We cannot deny what we experienced even though we cannot tell anyone. I'm just not sure Evelyn Murray ever existed at all."

Aerenthia shook her head in disgust before she asked. "How can you say such a thing? How can you think it after all we went through, and the years we spent with her? I knew Evelyn before Evelyn was her known name. Before your grandfather's grandfather was born. Don't tell me she didn't exist."

John explained. "I'm not trying to make you mad Aerenthia. Just hear me out. Time is different there. Even you did not know her when she was a child. And for Evelyn Murray, time doesn't count. There was never an Evelyn Murray... However, there was an Evelyn Starlight Porter. She didn't leave Adierach to escape a king... Not with her power. She crossed the ice to bring you to Anglamora. She came to my aunt Katie Carpenter when she was a child so one day, I would trust her enough to follow her to Anglamora."

Aerenthia was still somewhat confused as she asked. "You think she did all this so we would be together? To give her a new life?"

John answered with a question. "Do you remember how you became a wandering star or any time before that?"

Aerenthia replied. "I don't. I was always a star. At least as long as I can remember."

"In her eyes you most certainly were. I think, before you were a star, you were her mother. Mother, Aerenthia, is God in the eyes of a child. In her time loop, you were always her light in dark places. A day will come Aerenthia when she will walk out into that forest, and that old gate will open for her." John explained as he took Aerenthia by the hand.

Aerenthia nodded and said, "She all but said that very thing. It was on our wedding day when she and I talked alone."

John continued. "She used lightning and storms as her powers... We have to teach her Aerenthia. We have to teach her how to be the most powerful mystic who ever lived. We must teach her to be the eighth inspiration."

Aerenthia leaned against John and wrapped her arms around him. With her head against his chest, she responded.

"Tomorrow is her eighth birthday. Fate said it was on her eighth birthday when they came to her."

John held Aerenthia tight as both returned to looking at the stars in the night sky. John kissed Aerenthia's forehead before he said in a low voice, "I know why they call you Starlight."

From inside the house, young Evelyn was looking out of her window at her parents in the yard. Her starlight eyes cast a bright glare when she looked up at the sky where John and Aerenthia were looking.

Aerenthia's white night gown seemed to glow in the night to young Evelyn. The little girl smiled and said to herself just above a whisper.

"There must always be a light on dark moon nights."

After her words, she went to bed and her parents walked toward the house. It was a near sleepless night for John and Aerenthia who had a lot on their minds. For young Evelyn, it was a very peaceful night and once again she had a dream.

When morning arrived, it was Evelyn who was up before her parents. At eight years old she made the morning coffee for her dad and blended mint tea for her and her mom. John had started Evelyn drinking the tea on their outings in the forest. Aerenthia didn't care for it, but never turned down a cup from Evelyn.

When the hot beverages were done, she woke them up. Evelyn climbed on the foot of the bed and began bouncing up and down as she called out.

"You can't sleep all day. Wakey, wakey. Isn't that what you say to me?"

John sat up just a little and smelled the coffee coming from the kitchen.

"Did you make coffee Evelyn?" He asked.

She replied. "Yes. You showed me how remember? I made tea for mom and me too. So get up."

Evelyn started pulling at the blankets but Aerenthia held on tight.

"I'll get up in a minute. You wait for me or your dad to pour your tea. I don't want you getting burned." Aerenthia said in her sleepy voice.

Evelyn replied. "Okay... Dad, I had that dream again about people calling out to me."

John pulled the blanket back and set at the edge of the bed. He asked while rubbing his eyes.

"Same dream huh. Anything different about it this time?"

Evelyn answered. "Yes. There were many people just standing around looking at the seven who were standing out in front. Dad..."

John replied. "What is it?"

Evelyn asked. "Why isn't there eight?"

Aerenthia immediately sat up and looked at John. Evelyn laughed at her morning hair before she continued.

"There were so many people just standing there. I couldn't help but wonder why wasn't there eight instead of seven standing out front?"

John said to her, "There isn't eight because seven are waiting for you to join them."

Evelyn replied. "What? Me an eighth inspiration."

John stood up and said, "I need some coffee."

He took off toward the Kitchen with Evelyn following him. Aerenthia got up and put her house shoes on due to the coldness of the hardwood floor. Then she joined the other two in the kitchen.

By the time she got there, John had already poured a cup for Evelyn and himself. They were sitting at the table next to one another. Aerenthia poured her cup and stood with her back against the sink.

Evelyn asked. "If I have that dream again, you think I should join the other seven?"

John stretched and yawned before he responded.

"Not just in your dream. In life Evelyn, you must always try to do good things and strive to be an inspiration for others. The greatest thing you can ever be is a light in someone else's darkness. To help them in their time of need. Do you understand?"

Evelyn replied. "I think so."

John looked at Aerenthia who was watching closely. He gave her a wink before he changed the subject.

"I feel like I'm forgetting something. Feels like something was special about today."

Aerenthia smiled and winked at Evelyn who put her hands on her hips and said, "It's my birthday."

John laughed and said, "Oh that's right. I'm sorry. I forgot to get you a present."

Evelyn shook her head and demanded. "Where is my present? Where are you hiding it?"

John took a sip of his coffee and got up. He told Evelyn to stay put while he went after the present from his room.

When he got back, he had something in his closed hand. He turned in his chair to face Evelyn and held out his hand. When she opened his hand, she gasped in disappointment.

"Is that it? What is it?" She asked.

John replied. "It's a wooden nickel. It's a very old, very special wooden nickel."

Evelyn again shook her head. She wasn't interested in it at all. She said to him, "You can't do anything with a wooden nickel. How is it special?"

John told her. "Look at it. It says one hug on it. This was given to me by a very special friend. Because hugs from those you love are priceless, it can't be bought with money. So this wooden nickel was made to buy a hug. Right now, I want to buy one from you, so I'll give you this nickel. When you want a hug from me, you can buy it with this same nickel. It's like a game really."

John handed her the nickel and got his hug. When he let go of her, he continued.

"Don't lose this Evelyn. I mean it. This is very special, and one day I'll tell you all bout it and where it came from. Now the rest of your presents are hidden in the feed bin out in the barn."

Evelyn took off toward the door. John smiled at Aerenthia who was still questioning everything that was taking place.

When Evelyn stepped outside, John said to Aerenthia. "I'll bet you anything she feeds the birds this morning."

Aerenthia replied. "I think you're right. Those chickens are her babies. Especially that rooster she carries around."

The door opened and Evelyn stepped inside with empty hands.

"No way you made it out there that fast Evelyn. Are you okay?" Aerenthia asked.

Evelyn explained. "There was a man outside. He was on a wagon."

Aerenthia turned around to look out of the kitchen window while John stood up and started toward the door.

"I don't see anyone Evelyn. Where did he go?" Asked Aerenthia.

Evelyn replied. "He took the trail behind the barn to the woods."

Aerenthia immediately joined John at the door as she told young Evelyn to stay inside. Halfway across the yard, John said a single word to Aerenthia. "Max."

Together they walked down the trail that was only a tractor trail into the woods. The rain the day before made the wagon tracks very clear in the mud of the forest trail.

They followed the tracks until they ended at the old gate Max had left them many years before. John and Aerenthia looked around but didn't see anyone. Aerenthia couldn't help herself. She had to try to open the gate. She swung it over to the left side and slowly pulled it back, but Anglamora did not appear on the other side.

She asked. "Why would he go across the yard and not let us see him?"

Aerenthia looked back down the trail as her eyes grew wide. John beat her to it when he said, "Evelyn... They needed us away from her."

John and Aerenthia ran back to the house and burst in the front door. Young Evelyn was fine as she stood in the middle of the living area. She stood with the white staff in her hand.

John and Aerenthia stood silent in shock and disbelief. The white staff was just as they remembered it. The egg shaped crystal was on top and the silver inlaid strips of the scythe swirled down the twisted shaft.

"An old woman gave it to me." Evelyn explained.

"Did she tell you her name?" John asked.

Evelyn replied. "No. She said you and mom would tell me about her and how to use this staff."

Aerenthia slowly took John's hand as she kept her eyes on young Evelyn.

"Think of what you love most, and that crystal will cast a light." Aerenthia told her.

John looked at Aerenthia with a slight grin as he remembered the night she came to him on the western mountain of Anglamora.

Young Evelyn stood silent looking at Aerenthia as she began to smile. The crystal began to cast a faint glow in the room.

"Who is she? Who is the old woman?" Evelyn asked.

Aerenthia replied. "She was the best friend I ever had."

John replied. "She was like a mother to me. She taught us, being a light in someone else's darkness is the eighth inspiration we should try to be. She was the best of us and oldest of them all."

Aerenthia added. "She was a mystic... The greatest and most powerful mystic who ever lived. With that very staff, she defeated a terrible darkness."

Young Evelyn pulled the elastic band from her hair letting hang down on the sides of her face. John and Aerenthia's hands gripped tight to each other when Evelyn took a stance and lowered the staff in front of her.

The crystal at the end of the staff began to glow at the same time a single small strand of blue electric came from Evelyn's hand and traveled down the swirl of the twisted shaft.

"What was her name?" The little girl asked.

John replied. "She was Evelyn Murray."

Another strand of electric began to travel down the shaft and the crystal shined a little brighter. At the same time, a few strands of Evelyn's hair began to rise.

"Mom, why wasn't there eight to stand between the light and darkness?" She asked.

Aerenthia replied. "Because seven are waiting for you to join them."

The End

Made in the USA
Columbia, SC
19 May 2024

35923292R00129